This book is due for return on or before the last date shown
above: it may, subject to the book not being reserved by
another reader, be renewed by personal application, post, or
telephone, quoting this date and details of the book.

HAMPSHIRE COUNTY COUNCIL
County Library   100% recycled paper

VOICES
FROM THE
WATERWAYS

For my friends

VERA DAWKINS & BARBARA SIMPSON-LEE

VOICES
FROM THE
WATERWAYS

JEAN STONE

SUTTON PUBLISHING

BRITISH WATERWAYS

First published in 1997 by
Sutton Publishing Limited · Phoenix Mill
Thrupp · Stroud · Gloucestershire · GL5 2BU
in association with British Waterways

British Library Cataloguing in Publication Data
A catalogue record for this book is available from the British Library

ISBN 0-7509-1351-7

 ™ ALAN SUTTON™ and SUTTON™ are the trade
marks of Sutton Publishing Limited

Typeset in 13/18 pt Perpetua.
Typesetting and origination by
Sutton Publishing Limited.
Printed in Great Britain by
Butler & Tanner, Frome, Somerset.

Contents

PREFACE

Britain has always been a seafaring nation, so it is not surprising that this love of water has extended to the inland waterways. These became valuable highways in their own right, used for the transportation of commodities of all kinds. The great rivers like the Thames, the Severn, the Humber and the Liffey remain the natural commercial waterways, the reclaimed land of the Broads has recovered over 200 miles of navigable river and the vast man-made web of canals that sprawl over the countryside were specifically designed for the commercial carriage of goods.

When thinking of the expansion of these waterways, thoughts turn to those great architects and engineers responsible for their development; however, without the more humble presence of the navvies, boat-builders, boatmen, lock-keepers, navigators and wharf-hands, this growth would never have been possible. These commercial highways were nurtured to maturity, but now have almost died, falling into a slow and sad decline, suffocated by the coming of arterial roads and railways.

Reaching the end of an era there remain but few survivors who can remember the time when the waterways were at their commercial peak and whole families worked together, however the old way of life continues to linger, if only in their memories. The following pages comprise a portfolio of men and women who have devoted their lives to the canals and rivers and, whatever their skills and whatever region they worked, they all have tales to tell. Most are now retired and they have been happy to disclose some of their earliest memories of good times and bad times, camaraderie and fun, competition and rivalry and even catastrophes.

Today we tend to look back and talk of the 'old days' being so much slower than modern life, but it was not so on the water. It was always a race against time – a race against the next man to get there first to pick up another load. Time was money and sometimes this meant working right through the night just to get a decent wage packet. Almost without exception these men have known difficult periods in their lives and make no secret of their fight for survival.

Each contributor could tell enough stories to merit a book devoted entirely to their own life, but I hope I have been able to capture their most treasured memories within these pages. I have endeavoured to record their reminiscences in their own words and sometimes quite bold and colourful language, allowing us to enter more fully into their world; a world which to most of us is secret and mysterious and looked upon with curiosity.

They were a hardy breed, used to working endless hours, often in bitterly cold weather, and many can remember a time when there were few home comforts to return to. Nevertheless, they seem to have few regrets and look back fondly upon those hard days. I would like to thank them for their part in this book, for without them it could never have been written.

Jean Stone

ACKNOWLEDGEMENTS

My thanks go to all those people who have so willingly shared the stories of their lives and so enabled the publication of this book.

I extend my thanks to Helen Davies of Cadbury's Bournville; Judith Walker of the Salvation Army Heritage Centre; Roy Jamieson of the National Waterways Museum; Denny Plowman of the Canal Museum, Nottingham; Gary Norcop of Johnson's Potteries; David Shepherd of Cawood-Hargreaves and Peter Walsh of the Guinness Ireland Group.

The quotation from *The Water Gipsies* by A.P. Herbert has been reproduced by kind permission of A.P. Watt Limited on behalf of Crystal Hale and Jocelyn Herbert.

I am also indebted to many friends and acquaintances who have helped in a variety of ways. Among them are Barbara Simpson-Lee, Claire Lofting, Linda Holman, my daughter-in-law Joanne Stone, whose criticism (both good and bad) has been particularly appreciated, Maurice Bolton for the loan of his personal archive of the Northern Waterways, Michael Seago, and Keith and Clare Taylor.

The author has tried to trace the copyright holders of all the photographs used in this book. In certain cases it has not been possible to trace the copyright holder. The author apologises if any copyright has been accidentally infringed.

CONVERSION TABLE

Shillings and pence and some illustrative decimal coinage equivalents

1d	½p	1s	5p
2d	1p	2s	10p
3d		3s	15p
4d	1½p	3s 6d	17½p
5d	2p	10s 0d	50p
6d	2½p	12s 6d	62½p
7d	3p	25s 0d	£1.25p
8d	3½p	30s 0d	£1.50p

Chapter One

THE BARGE CAPTAIN FROM KILDARE

JACK GILL

Jack Gill

Trams once rattled their way along the cobbled road from Dublin City towards Inchicore. As they leaned and swayed past St James's Street Brewery, those passengers on the open-air top deck could enjoy the rich, heady aroma of hops lingering on the breeze; a reminder that Irish porter, or Guinness as it is now known, meant 'bread and butter' to many families in that area, whether they worked in the brewery or carted the barley and barrels of beer along the waterway.

Further on from the brewery is Inchicore, the nucleus of the Irish transport industry. Here the manufacture of rolling stock, the coach-building trade which turned out trams and buses, and the car-assembly works, have all given employment to local craftsmen and changed the landscape from leafy countryside to busy suburb. Jack Gill has witnessed this change firsthand, for he has lived in this part of Dublin since he was a young man, working the Grand Canal which passes through this way.

'I was born on 29 November 1910, in a little place called Killina,

The custom house, Dublin. (The Guiness Ireland Group)

near Carbury in County Kildare.' Jack was more than happy to tell his tales about his life on the canal. For him, boats have always meant hard work, but he says the rewards made it all worthwhile. His colourful memories portray a man who has had a lifelong romance with the Irish canals and bears no resentment about any of the hard times that he endured.

His father had been a bargeman with his own horse-drawn barge, who turned to boat-building on Clydebank when times were hard and Jack grew up knowing that he would follow in the family tradition as a bargeman. In Ireland, family traditions are strong and generations of Irish canalmen followed their forefathers in the same job and some still do. The Lindleys are another family that have long been associated with the canals. Alan Lindley is the eighth generation of the Mitchell family to mind the lock at Rahan and to have lived in the lock-house there.

Jack begins to relate his tales which are made more fascinating by his compelling Irish accent and distinctive turn of phrase. 'My father used to build ships on Clydebank in Glasgow when we was small children. So when he came home on holiday, he brought us all over to Glasgow in 1915. Me mother fell into bad health and she didn't like Glasgow so he brought us all back again in 1919!'

Jack had always been one of the lads, taking life in his stride and enjoying whatever fun came his way. Even as a small boy he was in the thick of things. 'We were there, there on Clydebank for four years and I was going to school in Argyll Street. The day the First World War was over, on 11 November 1918, we got out of school and we carried sticks, and we carried planks, and there was a terrific bonfire in Blackburton Street, and the Kaiser and his wife were dressed-up together as "hugger-muggers", we called them, and they were hanging across the street on a rope and when the blazes went up, they fell down into it. And we all joined hands and sang songs around the fire, "I belong to Glasgow, dear old Glasgow town". That's right, I was handed a box of matches to light the fire. I was eight year old then.'

After this Jack's father travelled backwards and forwards following work. 'When things got slack on Clydebank he used to come home to Dublin and work his own horse-drawn barge and then they would be busy working at Clydebank, he'd tie her up, tie up the boat here and he'd go over again.'

Lock-keepers were given a patch of land to grow vegetables and the right to graze a cow, but Jack's father was his own master and his family had their own smallholding of six or seven acres of land. Therefore he

A lock-keeper's cottage, Dublin.

could be confident they would be well-fed during his absences. 'When me father would be away in Glasgow, me mother and me uncle would take care of it. We used to grow vegetables and to rear cattle and we used to rear pigs and we reared hens and ducks.'

Punctuated by pauses as he sipped his hot tea, Jack proudly continued his tales. 'I came with me father on his barge; I came with him in 1926. I was sixteen years of age and I was on the canal up to 1960. He carried everything in the line of sundries now, down to the shops, all down round the Shannon and the Barrow. Say we brought out a load of sundries, that would be tea, sugar, bacon and flour, and all this business in the barge and we'd deliver some of that to the first town of Yattonderry, the next town would be Daingean and the next town would be Tullamore. Finish and empty your barge in Shannon Harbour and you'd bring a load of timber or a load of turf back.

'I did the same job as me father did.' When things got slack Jack went over to Clydebank too. 'I went over in 1929 and I served me time as a shipwright. I put the decks upon the Queen Mary and I built her small boats and I was there the day she was launched out into the salt water. I had a sledge in me hand and I hit the wedge and I let her off!

'When I came home to Dublin in 1935, everything was slack. I thought me father's boat would be below at Ringsend, so the first place I went was Ringsend and there is a boat-building place there called McMellins and I saw this boat in at the box getting repaired and I went into the office and asked if there was any work. I told them what I could do and the shipwright said, "Yes, when will you start?" So I started right away, after a couple of days, when I'd got me old clothes and everything sorted out.'

Jack could not believe his luck. His first concern was to find a place to live and, feeling eager and prosperous, it was not long before he found himself a wife too. 'First I had to get lodgings and when I went down to Macken Street, this girl Molly Geraghty was in it. There were two sisters and they owned the house and they used to let it out in lodgings. So, when Molly's father and her brothers used to go down the country on the barge she used to go and stay with these two ladies and I got lodgings in it as well. She knew all that belonged to me and I knew all that belonged to her and that's how we got acquainted.

'I went down and asked if she would like to be engaged. I had a good bit of Scotch money, all red notes at the time, and when I went into the jeweller's shop to buy the ring, the girl look at me and she says, "You know this is Scotch money?" So I says, "Is it no use?" "Oh yes," she says, "it is use, but we don't see a lot of it." "Well now," says I, "ye can have that anyway," and I told Molly to go round the shop and have her own choosing of the ring. I was married in 1936 and we lived fifty-nine years of a lovely and happy life.' Sadly, Molly has recently died and Jack made a present of the ring to his niece on her twenty-first birthday.

The couple continued to live in Macken Street for a while and it was there that their first baby, Angela, was born. Jack continued to do well, however, and they were soon looking for a house of their own and they found one by the canal. It was a blessing for Jack not to have to make the same long walk between home and work that his father did. 'Me father, he often left the barge in St James's Street harbour of a Saturday evening and he'd get out, and the trains were very scarce at that time. There was no buses on the road then, but if he got the train to Carbury, he'd still have six miles to walk home, so instead of doing that, he used to start off walking from Dublin and he'd walk the whole way home, twenty-one miles. He'd be left at evening after tying up the barge at six o'clock and he'd be home about twelve o'clock that night. Yeah, a long walk after a good day's work. Yeah. He left the house about three o'clock on Monday morning and he'd walk back. He'd be back in St James's Street in Dublin here about eight o'clock. He'd be ready here for to load his boat, or empty her, whichever the case might be.

'Yeah, when we got together we came up to New Ireland Road in Rialto and we bought a house up there by Rialto Bridge and I was up after me own barge. I bought me own barge and after working for a while with her, I got another, and another, and I wound up with three barges.' The Rialto Bridge is not far from the suburban cottage where Jack now lives. It was still countryside then with tall green rushes growing along the canal and a resident family of swans but, more importantly, Jack got a turf bank up by the canal. 'I had it there all during the war and I only lived a few yards away. A turf bank, you know, is a certain amount of ground by the side of the canal, or it could be St James's Street harbour, or anywhere where you could put out the turf and stack it up. You call that a turf bank, where we stored a big, big heap of turf.

'There were certain wide places on the canal for turning a barge. There was a wide place below at Rialto Bridge where I had the turf bank and when I'd emptied me barge on to the bank, I could just turn her around and get back again.' Molly was a great help to Jack as she had learned the turf trade from her father and brother who had owned a turf bank at Boland's Mill. Now she could manage their bank while Jack was away, perhaps collecting another load of turf. 'We collected the turf at the lower end of Offal at the other side of Tullamore, a place called Orhin. It used to come down from the high hill, a great big bog and it used to come down in bogics, a big cradle like. And this cradle used to tip over and there would be two men there with two big peat forks, and they shovelled it into the barge. The barges carried 50 ton.

'At first they were wooden barges and they were horse-drawn and then we got steel barges and they had a Bolinder engine in them from Sweden and the horse was wiped out altogether. There were stables all along the canal. You'd do a certain day's work. You'd leave St James's Street Harbour down here in Dublin and you'd go out to Hazelhatch and you'd stay there for the night. You'd get up then the next morning and land in

Boland's flour mills. Molly Geraghty's father had his turf bank nearby.

Robertstown, out in County Kildare. And the next day you'd go down to the lower end of the Shannon and a tugboat used to get a hold of the horse-drawn barges and tow either up the Shannon or down the Shannon, and the horses remained in Shannon Harbour until we'd come back. There'd be a man there looking after them. I had one horse and he was called Billy and another, she was a female, and we called her Maggie. We used to go out sixteen hours a day with the horse barges.

The turf cutters. Turf was an important cargo for Jack Gill and many other Irish bargemen.

'Well then, when we got the motor boats there were two more men in that boat along with meself and if we wanted to travel all night, as we often did, I'd go to bed first and I'd sleep so many hours, three or four, then I'd get up and let the next man into bed. So, if we wanted to be in a certain place next morning, we'd have that barge there.

'There was no lamplight at all. No, nothing at all. We knew the way and the blacker the sky will be the brighter the water will be, so you would see the middle of the canal. The chimney on the boat, we called it the funnel, you'd just keep that straight in the middle and you'd go through bridges and Acre Docks and all and you'd never rub them. We were up to all the knicks and knacks.

'Our barges were all black and there was a washboard going right round the belter with our name on it and her number as well. The barges had no names, they had numbers. The first barge I had was 106.B

Barge 64.M passing through a lock with a cargo of porter. (The Guinness Ireland Group)

and the second was 31.B and the next was 119.B. They all went by Bs and The Grand Canal Company had a whole harbour of boats and they were called Ms.' 'B' stood for 'Bye-trader' and this meant that Jack was required to pay tolls to the Grand Canal Company which covered both the lock fee and the commodities they carried.

'I carried everything as well. I carried coal, turf, tea, sugar, bacon, flour, pollack, barley and wheat, and of all things Guinness. We did a load of beer from Limerick and a load of timber back, or a load of turf during the war for the fires.'

In the latter half of the nineteenth century the Guinness brewery grew to such a size that it almost became a city within the city of Dublin itself and Jack was as pleased as Punch when he was able to get on a Guinness run, carrying a load of beer to Limerick or barley to the brewery. He remembers the 'perks' were good too. 'We always had Guinness from the brewery. When we'd go into Guinness with a load of malt or a load of barley, you used to get a bit of paper called a scrip and you'd go down into the tap room and you'd get a free pint of beer on that bit of paper. When you'd go to Tullamore, or Daingean, or Shannon Harbour, or any part of the Shannon, when you put out a load of beer the publican 'ud give you free drink as well.'

However, it is well known that some men, perhaps not eligible for a 'scrip', would make no bones about drilling a little hole in a barrel to drain off a pint or two and then carefully stop the hole with a wooden peg which would be painted and polished to conceal their dark deed!

Eventually the oak casks were replaced by metal barrels and the gentle horse-drawn barges by the world's beer-tanker ships, but right up until 1961, hordes of small boys would mockingly call from the banks and bridges to the captains on the barges, making their relatively short journey from brewery to port: 'Hey Mister! Bring us back a parrot!', mockingly implying the barges were going to travel to distant lands.

Women were not usually found on barges in Ireland; it was not considered the 'done' thing. 'The reason for that is this; them barges in England were all covered in, but we had to carry loaden. Neither me mother nor me wife would go on the barge. Well, me mother often got down in the cabin for to wash it and to clean it of a Saturday evening and me own wife done the same when we were there in St James's Street, but the wives did not go with the barges.'

This was no doubt why Jack became such a good cook and hospitable host. It could be lonely being away from home, so various crews would often congregate on his barge. 'We had a fireplace and we had a pot and we'd boil cabbage and potatoes. We had thump . . . you'd call it now. Mashed potatoes and leek, all mashed up fine. Thumped together with a knob of butter. Or we'd get steak and make soup. We had a pan and we had fried eggs and sausages or chops, or whatever the thing might be, and we used to bake our own bread. Well, indeed, when three or four barges would get together at night-time, they'd be out in the pub and we'd have a few drinks and we'd come back into the cabin. Maybe I would put on the griddle and I'd bake a cake and while the cake would be baking, there would be three or four men sitting around there and they would all be telling stories.

'I was going down to Waterford one day and it was a hard day in January and I had to catch the tide and this man was minding the lock in Gradner Manor and he was a bit of a poet, and a good one too, and he said to me, "Jack, I'm going to write a little song about this trip, be looking out for it upon the *Leinster Leader*". That's the paper out in Kildare. So he wrote the song all right. I'll tell it to you now:

I met aboard a motor boat one hardy son of toil,
And he gave to me a welcome of that grand old Irish style,
He told me he was Captain and he had as fine a crew,

As ever sailed the Grand Canal or wages ever drew.

He said it does not matter now what way this weather looks,

I have got to steer this little boat to the grassy Acre Dock,

And from that I rest to Robertstown and when she reaches there,

I'll take my helm once again, said the boatman from Kildare.

We'll sail down to the Shannon boy, her course is straight and wide,

Not like the old River Barrow where a man must catch the tide.

Give me Lough Derg, this lovely lake and I steer my passage through,

Or I'll anchor in the harbour at far off Killaloe.

And from that town down to Limerick, a straight course we must go

For the Shannon Navigation they changed the river flow.

And to look into this man-made lock, it might give you a scare,

Or change the face of nature, says the boatman from Kildare.

So when we get a night at anchor, we all sit round the fire,

And we tell our stories up and down to find out the greatest liar,

As every man is meeting a ghost, of sizes short and tall,

There must be one at every lock if you could believe them all!

For I said, I don't believe in spirits and their stories I do mock,

For its just as hard to find a ghost as the man who minds the lock,

And if any poor soul had wisdom and for his comfort care,

He'd keep far away from the Grand Canal, said the Captain from
Kildare.

'There was tin whistles, banjos, tambourines, and there was fiddles galore. I didn't play nothing. I sung. We went down to Milford one time when a big shipload of wheat came in from England and we brought it down. We were stowing it in a big store down in Milford, in the County Carlow, and there were four boats there along wi' me and we heard tell of this little pub in the village after getting in her cigarette supply and her beer supply. So the whole four crews went down into this pub this night. So we played and we drank nearly everything the woman had. They were two sisters and I sang a couple of songs anyway, and I sang a Scotch song called "The Girl I Left Behind". And when we were all coming out that night, meself and the chap that was with me, the lady was standing at the door letting us all out near twelve o'clock and she caught me by the arm and "I want to see you" she says, "when the house is empty." So, I turned round to me mate and I said, "Sure we didn't do anything wrong?" "No," he said, "we didn't." So I stood back anyway and when the last person had left the pub she said, "Will you follow me down into the kitchen?" So we went down and there was a lovely white tablecloth and a rasher and egg and sausages and a pot of tea on it. And I looked at the lady like and I said "Miss Commerford," I said, "this is a terrible great surprise for me tonight, I thought I was in trouble." "Now sit down and enjoy that meal of food," she said. "You're going to get another surprise now, because I want you to word me that song that you sung, 'The Girl I Left Behind'." She said she wanted it for her niece in Australia, if you believe that, so it's over there now. Oh, we had a grand night.'

Hidden beneath Jack's tough and hardy exterior is a kind, good-hearted man who is always kind to his horses and always accompanied by a dog. His kindness to a little dog when he was a boy he saw as being repaid many years later by him keeping a limb which he might otherwise have lost.

'I was travelling up from Ringsend one day and I threw out the rope. There was a post beside the canal and there was another man there. He dropped down the rope on the post. The coil of the rope was on the deck and the boat kept travelling and me foot was inside of the coil and she closed the rope and cut me foot right across. I went down to the

Patrick Dunne's hospital, in Grand Canal Street, and the doctor, when he looked at it said, "I'm going to amplicate [amputate] this foot." Says I, "Now tell me what you mean by that?" "Well, take it off, there is nothing but a bit of skin holding it." "Well," I said, "leave it on. You put a plaster of Paris on that and tighten it up," says I. I was only a young man at the time, twenty-six years of age. So they put the plaster of Paris on it and they put an iron under me heel and he said to me, "We'll do it for you all right, but it will always be crooked" and I said, "No matter how crooked it would be, it would be better than a crutch." So I have it and I'm working and I'm carrying heavy loads on it since.

'The reason why I wouldn't let them take it off was this. When I was a little boy in the country, I used to go round catching rabbits with me little dog. The dog's name was Spot. And another man used to set traps for to catch rabbits. My little dog got his paw into this trap and it was hanging off and meself and me father got an elder stick, from an elder bush, and we cut it and we split it down and took the pith out of the middle of the stick and we made two little clamps and we laced up his leg with a piece of twine and do you know, that paw, it set and I hunted and caught rabbits with that dog after. And that's why I would not let him take off my foot.'

Jack went on working the canal until 1960 when it was finally closed down. He accepts that canal freight transport eventually had to finish, but his mind wanders down those lost avenues. 'All the water in St James's Street harbour, there was a big bay of water in there like a pond, it used to hold about 150 barges. Well, that's all filled up now and there's grass growing in it.'

Jack, however, is more resilient. Nobody can take away his memories and there is nothing he enjoys better than to recount the tales of his life on the Grand Canal. 'Just one more thing,' said Jack, a twinkle in his eye. 'Well now, about sixty years ago a man gave me a song on paper and he was from Carbury and he wrote this song. Well, there's a big river here in Ireland goes all through West Mayo, County Mayo and it goes through Kildare and it's called the River Boyne. Well, he wrote a song and he said:

When I was young I went off to fish in the noontime of the day,
Down by a brook my way I took and along the Boyne did stray,
It was there I seen a girl undressed and my frame she did compound,
So my line and hook went down that brook and it never yet was found!

Chapter Two

CANAL-BOAT WOMAN

ROSE   WHITLOCK

Rose Whitlock

'I'm seventy-nine year old now,' said Rose. 'I was born in a little house in Rickmansworth. Mam's family came from London and they had wide boats. They used to have about six of them behind a big tug. Me mam was on the boats and me dad was on the boats and then he got called up and he was in the army. He used to work for Dickinson's paper mills and he was what they used to call a paper dasher.' These men were specially selected to provide a fast service. 'Then, of course, they got this little house in Rickmansworth and I was born there.'

When Rose's father came out of the army he went to work for L.B. Faulkner until his father thought it was about time he had his own boats: 'I thought about getting a pair of boats for you, and an 'orse, and starting you up?' Rose's father talked to her mother about this and she said, 'Well, if they are going to be all right?'

'So he bought a pair of boats 'cos they weren't dear then and the horses weren't that dear and me dad started up to Dickinson's paper mills. I think we worked there ten or eleven years and we lived on the boats. I didn't go to school. I went to school about four or five times, but we weren't in long enough to learn. We went to school while the boats were waiting to load up and when the boats was loaded someone would come running down for you, "Come on we're loaded. We're ready to go." So off we went again and that bit we'd learned that morning, I'd forgotten by the time we went again. I had to steer a boat when I was nine year old and have a rope tied round me. Me dad used to tie a rope and there used to be a hole in the front of the doorway where he'd put a stud in to ease the rope along.'

Rose lived on the boat with her parents and her sister and when her aunt, the mother of seventeen children, died leaving a family of twelve, her cousin came to live on the boat too. 'In them days you wouldn't let any of them go in a home. One went to one aunt and uncle and one to another, so me dad decided to have Laura and that's how it went on.' Life continued in the same way, until Rose's father died in 1937. 'We'd still got boats of our own and me mam said, "Well, that's it. We've gotta work now to get a living." Ladies could work as long as you knowed what you was doing.

'My mam did legging (*see* pages 73–4). She used to tell us she'd done it, but we never did it. When I was a little girl I grew up with tugs, you see. Well, nearly all those with their own boats had converted to a motor boat so, of course, the tugs finished and we couldn't get through the tunnels. We'd only had a boat converted to a motor for about twelve months when me dad died, so the man who put the engine in showed me all about it. It weren't the engines they have now; touch a button and they're gone. You had to sort 'em out, take 'em to pieces. I used to sort it out sometimes if it weren't going very good at twelve o'clock at night. Get a bit of rag and undo the nuts. We went on twelve years without a man.'

Even after Rose got married she still had to carry on 'without a man' because her husband was called up to complete his National Service. 'Do you know, we used to go through the trees when there was only me and mam and Laura and me sister. Twelve o'clock at night, all through a big spinney at Watford Park. It's all big parks and we used to go through there. I used to have a pair of old trousers of me dad's on and a trilby hat. I was the man if anybody was about, but you never used to see a soul. But now, you daren't go from A to B.'

It was not unusual for the women to travel through the night and even on an ordinary night there were not many hours spent in bed. 'You used to go to bed at twelve o'clock at night and you were out at about four or five in the morning. You done nothing but work. If there was going to be a lock repair, we would probably go out all night so we could get through the locks before they closed and get unloaded, if we could. We would want to get unloaded and be back empty. Now if we didn't go out all night we should have been laid there loaded and had a load in for the whole weekend then.

'We used to go from Tamworth, Polesworth, Coventry, to the Ovaltine factory, Dickinson's paper mills and Curly & Tong's [Kearly & Tonges] at Southall. We used to carry coal, but during the war the government used to claim us. The government claimed us if they'd got any goods in the docks when the raids was on, to get it out. We used to take the coal that way, then the government made arrangements with the companies that if we was unloading up that end and they wanted the stuff out of the docks 'cos of the bombing, we used to have to go and get it out of the docks and take it back. We used to go to Birmingham with it. We used to be in Limehouse Dock with the doodlebugs going over and we'd got no man, only us women, me and me sister, me mam and me cousin.'

During the war years the government enlisted women trainees to work on the canals. Rose remembers that they had trainee men at one time too. 'They trained them, but they were hopeless. They nearly sunk a boat. It was a man's private owned boat, it was. 'Course, when they nearly sunk it, that finished 'em. They couldn't care less. It was fun to them. Then they had the trainee women, which was good. We got on all right with them. I learnt them to splice ropes and twingle the mops and all that sort of thing.' Rose explained further: 'We never wring a mop. We used to get it on our arms and twirl it to twingle all the water out. One girl, she came here to visit us the other day, it was like olden times, she got in with [married] the boatman and they worked a pair of boats, they did, for years.'

As well as managing the boat there were also the usual household chores to be carried out. Shopping wasn't difficult, as Rose said: 'I used to hop off on me bike and get me shopping. Come back again and probably they'd be loaded up ready. I'm not being funny or anything, but they were the bestest times of our life. We was our own boss. We could go on if we wanted to. We could stop if we wanted to. We could have a day off if we wanted to. But then we didn't get the money.

'In the war we had travelling coupons to go to any of the canal shops. A lot of the canal shops we had always gone to and they'd always help us out and let us have a bit more than what we should have. Then there used to be a man at Fenny that used to save us things. We did all right. Some of the boat people that had a big family, couldn't afford all the rations and me mam used to give them a bit of money and they would give us some extra coupons. They wanted the money and we wanted the coupons.' During the war years manual workers were allowed extra rations and Rose remembered: 'We got extra sugar and tea and cheese. The company we were working for, got that. And soap. They meant for us to have a wash after we'd loaded the coal,' she laughed.

Rose's cousin Laura, who still lives with her, joined in the conversation. 'Oh, yes, we got a bit black. We didn't have any big baths or showers like they got now. It was a treat really to have a nice bath.' Laura was sometimes able to enjoy a bath at a cousin's house, but the first bath Rose took was not enjoyable. 'Oh! I got frit to death when I got in the bath. I thought I was drownded!'

'Yes, she nearly passed out,' confirmed Laura.

'Yes, but we was always clean because we would get the bowl and somebody would come and wash your back where you couldn't get to and then you'd wash the other parts yourself. Then I used to say to my son, "Get you a blinking good wash." "I ain't with you staring," he said. I said, "I can soon sort that out." I used to pull the slide over and shut the door and steer in the hatches so nobody didn't see him. I used to get that bowl, "Now let me rub your back." 'Course, he got the towel holding up the front on him and me rubbing his back and steering the boat, then the rest of it he did himself.

'I used to dress the kids going along. One of our friends used to feed her baby going along. Hold the baby, breast-feed the baby and steer with her back, you know. Her husband wouldn't stop. He was a bit mean. Ever so mean. He wouldn't stop while she fed the baby. He's ever such a lovely lad now.'

There was also the problem of washing clothes and getting them dry. 'We used to have miles and miles of clothes because we couldn't wash 'em every week. We used to shove 'em in a bag and shove 'em in the front end of the boat 'cos we hadn't got the room and when we got stopped of a weekend, it might be at Curly & Tong's, where we'd got to unload, or might have to load up, and we used to get the old dolly tub out and the mangle out and wash all these clothes up. We used to have lines and lines of washing about, and pegs, and all to get it dry. We used to tie them along the trees and we used to tie 'em along each boat if there were no trees. Pull what we call the mast up and take the line back to the tiller, then take it down to the stud and tie it and have the line prop under it and that's how we used to do it. Now Curly & Tong's had a shed affair, where two men used to mend the barrels and if it were a wet day, we used to get under this shed, have the fire bucket outside, and get under this shed with the mangles and the bowls and the buckets, all under this little shed. Then when we was finished, we used to sweep it all out and clean it all out and then the men used to come the next morning and they'd say, "You done some washing the weekend didn't you?" 'Cos the little shed was clean!'

If the weather had been wet and they could not get the washing dry at the weekend, then they would dry it on the boat as they went along. However, this was not so easy in the winter when there could be many different problems.

'It was a bit hard in the winter,' went on Rose. 'It was all right if you were loaded with coal because you could keep making the fire up. We got frozen up on the Ashby Canal for about twelve weeks. Dad had to

Laura Carter (the little girl, second on the right) with her mother and family.

walk ten mile to a labour exchange and he got about £2 10s and that had to keep us for a week and he had to walk ten mile to get it. An' then when they come to break the canal, they had thirteen horses. Ashby Canal belonged to the Great Central Railway in them days and then they nationalized all the canals. They had thirteen horses and the ice was thirteen inches thick. They had all the horses and the ice-breaker and all the horses pulled the ice-breaker on top of the ice and then they had to pack up 'til it thawed a bit. They tried to rock it, but it was on top of the ice. That was in 1929. We was still froze up in May.

'The last time we got frez up a long time was Hemel Hempstead. 1962 to '63. We was froze up there for ten weeks. We had to sign on the labour. There's things we look at, and there's books we look at when we have a boat show down here at Braunston and them books are more money than we used to get when we worked. We couldn't live on the money now. 'Cos all we used to get, by the time the stamps was taken out, we used to get about £10 10s. The thing was, we didn't have any light to pay for, we didn't have any rent to pay for, we didn't have any poll tax to pay. We didn't have anything to pay after the stamps was paid, except to keep ourselves.'

When they were children, the girls would try to find ways of earning themselves some pocket money and Laura remembered that this could be very hard work. 'When I was about eleven or twelve, I used to go in the trucks with Rose's sister and we used to shovel the coals out. Of course, when the men at the pit had knocked off after their shift they'd do the boats' loading up. Well, if we wanted to get loaded up quickly they sent the coal down to alongside the boat and we used to tap the doors and put a shoot on and let the coal down. Then me and her sister used to get in the wagon and shovel it down. We used to load a boat sometimes before the men come. Sometimes we got one boat loaded and the men used to be pleased 'cos we'd done it and we'd be away early. They used to give us a bit of money for that, because they used to get extra pay. "Oh, you be devils" they used to say.'

'At one time they emptied the coal with skips, like a bucket,' joined in Rose. 'They used to ease it down into the boat and then they had to shovel all the coal into it and then they'd hang it on again and take it out, but for the last few years they had a grab and they grabbed it out. Early on we were loaded from railway trucks, but the last part we were loaded with lorries. They'd knock the back up and shoot it out.'

'We've done some work, but then we were very happy,' they agreed.

Rose remarked on the presence of bollards at the locks today, but complained, 'while now you tie the boats up in a few minutes, we had to knock the stakes down with an iron sledgehammer. Used to have to jump off the boat with those, and knock 'em down and then take 'em up again in the morning. They've got ladders up the sides of the locks now. We had to jump down the locks, not get down the ladder, and the locks are automatic now; we had to open 'em all.

'Bill, my husband, was the bikeman. He used to grumble that he did all the lock-wheeling, but he had the easiest job. His bike is in the museum at Stoke Bruerne now. He had it from the tip place at Berkhampstead where they used to tip all the rubbish. All the boat people used to go there when they wanted another bike. There used to be a man there and if you give him five bob and give him a drink, you know you'd get a good bike. He was always changing bikes. Well, he had that Raleigh bike for all them years and then he gave it to the museum. They've got the bike clips and the 'lastic on the saddle at the back where he used to put his rain-mac on. I thought it was nice to keep it in there for olden times.'

Pleasures were rare for those people who worked on the canal, but they took great pride in the interior of their narrow boats. Space was limited, but they were usually painted in the traditional style with 'roses and castles', there would be plates hanging on the walls and a brass collection. Great care would be taken of all these decorations. After many years of cooking on the little range, Rose decided to try a paraffin stove. 'When you cooked the food on that, just one heat, it didn't boil over. Just cooked the food slowly. I had a cardboard box as went round, so it didn't burn the paintwork each side.'

Their brass collection received regular attention. 'We had brasses. There was one or two things we used to keep. We used to keep brass bed-knobs for decoration, for show. We used to go to Berkhampstead and the man there that had the scrapyard, where we used to get the bikes, he used to have all sorts and we used to get the brass off him. We used to have the brass knobs off the bedsteads and we used to have brass handles on the drawers. We wouldn't let the children polish the brass because they used too much brass paste. So we used to do them ourselves. There's a knack in brassing. If you put too much brass paste on, it dries all in the cracks, so we never used to put much on, else you would collect a lot of Brasso in the cracks in the brass work.

'We collected the hanging-up plates too. There was a lot about in those days. I used to bike from Bedworth to Coventry and somebody used to say to me, "Get some of them Coventry hanging-up plates" and I used to go there. They used to have the Coventry three spires on. I've biked from Bedworth to Coventry many a time and brought about six pairs back for different people. Sixpence ha'penny each. Me aunt used to put ribbon through, but we didn't because we used to get them down and wash 'em quick.' Rose pointed to a plate hanging on her kitchen wall, 'That one up there is a very old plate. That come from Oxford Woolworth's.

'Some people used to tie horse's tails on the boats as part of the decoration, but we didn't. People we know that went to Banbury, they always had one. Sometimes it was a horse's tail and sometimes it would be a cow's tail, if it were a nice cow's tail. If it were a white one, you know. I'm not being funny or anything, but all the cows now, they don't seem to have any nice tails.

'I never had a big Meacham teapot, but I had two little ones. Miniatures. Big families used to use the big Meacham teapots. There used to be a shop and it used to have two little windows. One window had the Meacham teapots, kettles, cups, basins, all in and the other side was a sweet shop, and it was on the bridge at Meacham. They were brown and they had all got the figures on, but the big Meacham teapots, with the little teapot for the knob on top of the lid, they used to be 7s 6d. They are about £200 now.'

Unsurprisingly, there was little time for socializing in their busy lives. Laura says she did not have a boyfriend until she was eighteen and then they, 'went to the pictures down at Uxbridge. Then after that, if we passed one another and it wasn't tying up time we'd go on and he used to come back on his bike. Then he would have to bike back to his own boat again.'

However, there were opportunities for meeting their friends and relations if there was a gathering at a pub. 'We used to go in the pub at Hawkesbury Stop. We'd got no money and so we'd have half a pint of shandy. Then somebody would come up and play the old 'cordian and then everybody put 3d and fill the ol' water can with beer and have a couple of tots and that was how we used to go on. Everybody had a drop. They weren't how they are today, everybody got to have pints and pints and pints. We used to have a little drop of beer and our mam used to be out there singing. Didn't she Laura?'

'Yes, we had a good old time,' replied Laura. 'Yes, and somebody had a melodian. My brother's got one now. It's bigger than a concertina and he plays it to all his children.'

'One chap has a 'cordian,' said Rose, 'he has a piano accordian and he can't read or write. He's seventy-odd now, and if a song comes out on the radio, he can play it on his 'cordian. He plays beautifully on his 'cordian. He gets it on the boat down there and he plays away there. Since he got redunded off the boats, he's got one of the pleasure boats now, he don't come out. He ent been to any shops since he's been here. Since 1970. But he gets his 'cordian out and he plays.'

It was a sad time for all the canal-boat people when work finally ceased. Although Rose and Bill had heard rumours and had been expecting the end for nearly two years, when the news did come they could not believe their ears. It was soon to be confirmed.

'It was Sunday, 13 October 1970. I'll never forget the date. We come down here in the morning and me uncle come in the afternoon and me son went up to see his Aunt Rose and when he come back he said, "Mam, Aunt Rose has just told me the jam factory has finished." "No, she always said we would be going there on a walking stick," I said, taking her off sort of thing. Then Ern come along and he said, "Rose do you know the jam ole's finished?" That was Curly & Tong's factory. "No," I said, "we shall be going there on a walking stick," I said, taking his mam off. "No, putting all joking to one side, it is."'

Rose went to see the manager at the yard, Mr Street. He had not been notified by the coal contractors, but he said he would enquire the next morning.

Rose continued her story. 'I went back to see Mr Street. "Good morning, Mrs Whitlock. You're right. I've been on to them this morning. It's finished. They've got a stock of coal and they've got to wait until they've used the stock of coal and then they might want a bit more by boat."

'We had six weeks laying there, then we took another load, but the canal had all silted up. Where we got the coal from was all quarries and they let all the rubble in the canal. They've stopped it now. The pleasure boats washed it from the sides to the middle, but all on it had settled and we had a job to get through. It took about three days to do about three hours' work. We was the last coal carriers to go along. When we stopped for those six weeks, it got so solid we couldn't do it. They pulled the boat on top of the mud. You could see the propellers, no water round them. Well, what could I say? We did look a sight. On top of this mud with a big tractor pulling us.'

It was a sad end to what had been a very happy way of life. Now they had to start all over again. With their hard-earned savings they bought a boat to live on, but life was not easy for Laura. 'I had to sleep in what you might call a tent. I slept under a tarpaulin on a butty boat. I parted it all off and made it into a little place and I had a bedstead in there. I slept there for six years. It used to be a bit cold in the winter, but we had a stove and a cooker. Then me things started to go a bit damp and I kept moaning and groaning.' Rose and Bill had difficulty filling in the forms to apply for a house, but eventually they sent them off and they got the council house in Braunston.

Rose found work cleaning camping boats. 'I had to do something and that was my delight.' Laura, however, did not find it so easy to get work. As she could not read or write, she found herself doing strenuous manual work. Rose still has a lot of sympathy for Laura. 'She had to do a man's job, working with men. She worked at concreting and cementing. Everything. Put petrol pumps in. Everything.'

However, Rose and her husband and Laura settled in the new house, the only problem being that Rose could not sleep. For all those years she had lived on the boat, she had always slept on a flock mattress which was folded up as soon as she got up in the morning. Now she says, 'I couldn't stand the springs in the mattress so I slept on the floor.' Eventually she was given some good advice by her cousin: 'Do the same as I did . . . I put my boat bed on. Have you still got yours?' So Rose collected her flock mattress from the boat. 'We shook it all up, aired it and put it in a clean tick and put it on the bed. I had it on for quite a while then Laura said, "There ent half a lot of dust come out of them flocks." So I took it and made some pillows with it and then I got used to the springy mattress.'

Rose and Laura are enjoying life again now, although they still think their best days were spent on the canals. Rose's son and daughter live and work nearby and plenty of family members, old friends and acquaintances live in the area. Braunston is one of those busy, happy places where people from the canals have finally settled.

THE FIELDINGS AND THE *SALVO*

When Fred Fielding was a child, his parents owned a shop just off the High Street of New Bradwell in Buckinghamshire. The canal-boat families would often call in for groceries and, as a boy, Fred became fascinated with their way of life. Many years later, in 1929, when Fred was an officer in the Salvation Army, he married Ivy Copping. They worked together during the Blitz in London and Liverpool and, like most people, dreamed of more peaceful times to come. They decided that when the war was over, they would like to be involved in improving the welfare of the canal-boat families. Fred had had a comfortable childhood and he had never forgotten those he considered to be his less fortunate friends.

When they heard the sound of the Salvation Army band playing nearby on Sunday evenings, the canal-boat children, often followed by their mothers, used to leave their boats and go along to listen to the music and perhaps join in the singing. On one chilly November day in 1950, however, on the wharf at Water Eaton, the occasion was even more exciting: the music hailed the launching of a boat, the *Salvo*. This was a narrow boat, freshly painted in traditional canal designs, but, curiously, instead of the usual company logo painted on the bows, there was the Salvation Army shield and a cross. People were puzzled that this boat should have a cabin in its bows big enough to seat twelve to fourteen people. It was well known that Salvationists had been visiting bargees along the canals since the turn of the century, but never before had they owned their own narrow boat. This particular 72-ft wooden-hulled narrow boat had been purchased by the Salvation Army at Fred's request.

Some canal-boat people were already friendly with the Brigadier and

Brigadier and Mrs Fred Fielding on board canal boat Salvo.
(The Salvation Army International Heritage Centre)

his wife whom they had often met along the canal side. They thought it strange that they should have turned to a life afloat, but they were a little shy in asking what it was all about.

Nevertheless, it was not long before the children were welcomed aboard and were soon sitting in the large cabin, which contained a song roll, chairs, pictures and all the other things found in a Salvation Army meeting hall. Here they enjoyed films, slides, puppet shows, learned songs and joined in choruses and some children said their prayers for the first time. The song roll, however, was of limited use. The Fieldings discovered that some children were unable to read and write. They were obviously intelligent and very accomplished in the skills of boating but, always on the move, they had no opportunity to go to school. However, Fred and Ivy Fielding took up the task of giving simple lessons in reading, writing and arithmetic. They were always there to help the bargees, sometimes providing clothing or perhaps helping with letter writing or form filling; first aid was available and occasionally they even helped deliver babies.

The children looked forward to the days when *Salvo* would be moored near them so that they could visit the Fieldings. Each child was the proud owner of a membership card with a photograph of *Salvo* on the front and 'Jesus – Friend of Little Children' written on the inside. There is no doubt that all the children enjoyed belonging to this 'club', for it was a wonderful opportunity to meet their old friends, make new ones and join in plenty of exciting activities. Canal life could be quite lonely for some children as there was little in the way of organized community amusements in which they could participate.

Mrs Fielding gives a geography lesson on board Salvo *(The Salvation Army International Heritage Centre)*

There was a Sunday school, but no set time for meetings. The bargees would come and go according to their own particular timetables, but it would not be unusual to see Fred, lantern in hand, picking his way along the tow-path to make the acquaintance of a family in a newly arrived boat. Often he would return with a group of children to hold a 'Joy Hour' when they would participate in the various activities which would sometimes continue until after nine o'clock. 'We do not need to recruit them, they are very keen and come when they can,' the Brigadier remarked, and it is said that many bargees showed their gratitude by painting two red rings on the black chimneys of their barges, to indicate that Salvation Army members were welcome aboard.

During the winter months, *Salvo* was taken off the water, but the good work continued in a small hut at Hawkesbury Junction, near Coventry, which opened every evening as a very popular youth centre. However, it was the children's Christmas party that was the highlight of the year. The date of the party would travel at lightning speed along the canal web and busy fathers would be cajoled into travelling all night long to get their youngsters to the party on time. Some years there would be more than 450 children there and presents collected by churches and chapels near and far would be given to each one.

So successful was the work of the Fieldings that when *Salvo* became worn beyond repair, she was replaced by a new wooden-hulled narrow boat, *Aster*, donated by the British Waterways Commission who considered the couple's work with the canal people 'invaluable'. Fred and Ivy Fielding continued carrying the gospel along 2,700 miles of waterways until the 1960s.

Chapter Three

FIRST AND LAST ON THE NARROW BOATS

E D W A R D   W A R D

Edward Ward

Edward Ward lives in a terraced cottage in the suburbs of Coventry, the heart of the canal country where he once travelled and worked on the narrow boats. His daily toil is still on the canals, but now each day he makes a journey to the site where he works as a dredger, or 'mud-'opper' as these men are known along the waterways. Back in his comfortable sitting room on the chimney breast above the fireplace, is a collection of brightly polished brasses, a reminder of the days when a narrow boat on the canal was home.

His relations were part of an old canal-boat family and Ted says his grandfather died a young man, but he can still remember his grandmother. 'She died, say thirty years ago, [but] they wouldn't let me Grannie carry on, because you had to have a man in charge of the boats. That was British Waterways, the Grand Union Canal Carrying Company's, and Fellows, Morton and Clayton's rules, so she had to let her son take charge of the boats and she was with the son right 'til the time they packed up in, say, 1951. There was no way out on it for a woman, if the bloke died you either had to get someone else to rent his boat for ye, or pack up, in those days.

'My parents used to have four boats. They used to be in charge of the narrow boats, yes, but it was for a firm. If they had owned the boats they would have been called 'Number Ones'. The reason why my family worked for bigger firms . . .', Ted thought carefully and then explained. 'I mean, it wasn't a lot of money to maintain boats in those days, but we wasn't getting paid a lot of money. Now if a Number One boat had a wood plank go [break], right down the boat, it would probably take them three months to pay for it to be repaired. That's how poor the wages was. Whereas British Waterways and Fellows, Morton and Clayton, they had big fleets of boats so they would do their own repairs and these big companies started to push these small companies out, and they had no choice but to sell up.'

An inn at West Drayton showing a barge owned by Thomas Clayton. Perhaps Ted's father and grandfather rested their horses here.

Ted was born in Uxbridge, but has spent his life living in various parts of the country and travelling the canals. 'Our family lived on their boats and, as a child, I lived on a boat and I liked it very much. Mother did all the cooking on the boat. It was a hard life for any boatwoman. They didn't only have to do the cooking and the cleaning, they had to also help to work the boats, because it was a family concern.'

The children played an active part in running the boats too, but they didn't look upon this as a chore. It was a life they were used to and had been brought up to accept and enjoy. 'Your role would be . . .', Ted paused as he recaptured those childhood days, 'they'd teach you how to steer a boat for a start off, at an early age, and then they would set you off getting the locks ready for the boats to travel into, so they would gain time. You would get off the boat with the push-bikes, and when the locks wasn't close together you'd go on to the next lock and get the lock set for the boats to come into. It would gain you about ten minutes every time you got to a lock. Those days you didn't have to close any locks behind you, but you do now because it's all changed for pleasure craft. Another thing, as a youngster you could end up, as the boats unload, pushing the boats out and rolling the sheet covers up. All sorts of things they'd have you doing.'

The children's pleasures were modest and simple, but were obviously enjoyed with great gusto as, without a doubt, Ted thoroughly enjoyed recounting his childhood memories. 'I went to the Salvation Army as a kid. It was something new at the time. The people, the Fieldings, they had two boats and they were quite well in with boating families because these two boats had little classrooms. They used to collect all the boat children up to go and sing hymns and all that. I used to go and I thought it was good at the time. It was definitely entertainment.

'There was a mission at Brentford too for the boat children and also, for the town children, there was a proper chapel. There was a bloke down there and for all the years that I can remember, he was involved with the canal people, and he used to do a service in the town, in Brentford High Street. And I can tell you what! Some of the boat children were that good singers, hymn singers, they were better than town people, 'cos we could sing the hymns over the top on 'em and they didn't like it, but some of them we used to get on with quite well and it was good. I'll tell you, I have been in the back of the chapel many a time and I have heard all the boat children over the top of the other ones and the hymns have been really great. We have had good times.

'There was a big family of us. There was fifteen in our family. They had a school at Brentford and Bull's Bridge, but at Bull's Bridge they had like a school-boat. The earlier generations, they had a couple of days here or a day there. They never had like a proper schooling. The ones with the parents that was quite clever, they used to teach the kids of a night-time for an hour or two, but British Waterways had a better idea and they had this boarding school at Erdington, Birmingham, and when us children was old enough we went for the season. So you didn't have all your childhood on boats. The Waterways paid for this schooling and everything. I went to Erdington. Nearly all us lot and half the wife's family, they all got in there and they all got good jobs.'

Ted was the eldest of the children and he agreed that many responsibilities fell on his shoulders. 'That's why when I was sixteen I started on my own, in charge of my own boats like. My father used to work for Fellows, Morton and Clayton and the generation before him was on Grand Union Canal Carrying Company and that's how it all started off, through the families. I was working, after I left school, with me father on British Waterways, because the canals was nationalized. Fellows, Morton and Clayton were took over and when I was old enough, sixteen year old, in 1958 I was one of the youngest Captains to ever take out, in charge of a pair of commercial boats. Well, in those days, me father, if he signed for you to have a pair of boats, you could take in charge of boats at sixteen. If not, you had to be twenty-one. That was the rules of the game for British Waterways. Anyhow, I took in charge. I was very nervous, you know. You imagine all sorts of things were going to happen to the boats and yourself, but then things got better as they went on. We didn't have any serious accidents. We had minor ones, but if you had a serious one, you'd never get another job on the canals.

'When I was sixteen, there was two on us. The other lad was round about the same age as meself. A chap from a big boating family, they was an' all, and the kid who worked wi' me was called John Bess. He come on a few months and left. Ooh, he done that for about three times like and then he got married, like meself at the end of the day, like. We enjoyed it and it was the faster you went, the faster you earned money.

'You would start off where you had the boats from, Bull's Bridge Depot, Southall, and they'd find out whether or not you were good enough to do the job, for a start off. They would put you on a short run, from Brentford to, say, Boxmore, with a load of lime juice, or they would send you with a load of wood pulp from Brentford, Middlesex or Limehouse Docks to John Dickinson's, either to Croxley Green or Nash Mills and that would be your first run and they would see how you done the run. If you were quite fast enough, then you would be on big runs, and probably the next run, you would be to Birmingham or Wellingborough with a load of loose grain.'

Ted was very keen to emphasize how important it was to work hard 'to get ahead' and make good time. Time was one of the most important considerations when working on the cut.

'If you were on a long run you would load up at Brentford, or say the Regent's Canal Docks, and you would go to Birmingham Depot. Well, those days the normal working time would be over a period of five days.

At Bull's Bridge in the 1950s. Left to right, Mr Kalelane, Alf Hambridge, George Radford, George Wain, Ron Hough, Ted Ward, Ann Lane. (National Waterways Museum)

You used to start early in the morning, so if you were paying someone, like I was, a mate, someone younger 'n yourself, it was up to you not to do it in five days. You would do it in three days. So you would start off, load your first pair of boats by ten o'clock in the morning and you would sheet the load up and you would probably set off by dinner time. You would work 'til nine or ten o'clock the first night and you'd be going again about three to four o'clock in the morning. You'd be going all day and you had your food on the move and some people used to wash on the move.

'Then you'd get to Birmingham in three days if you were lucky. The Birmingham Depot knowed if you was a good working person by how fast you travelled from London to Birmingham, and if you were a good person, you'd load back from the goods warehouses the same day and get straight back to London. Inside the seven days you could be back in Brentford or Regent's Canal Dock and complete the round trip. But if you was a person that was not a good person, they would send you back round to the coal pits to load up for John Dickinson's, or anywhere. Then you would have one day travelling from Birmingham to the coal pit. If you were lucky you would load on the second day from the day you had unloaded and then you would go back to John Dickinson's in three days. Then you might end up a week waiting to unload. So it's up to yourself. If you wanted to prove yourself, it was up to you to do it, but if you wanted to lose money, if you was just in it for pleasure, you could take from there 'til Christmas, like.

'Every minute counted, you couldn't afford to waste time. Those days there wasn't many people had friends 'an all, because you would be in a pub with them and laughing and joking and having a drink with them, but once you left the pub everyone was for themselves. It's competition, right?

'There was these jobs and there was loads of competition, because there was all these little private firms, these Number One companies. They thought they had priority over the canals, but the priority over the canals, and it still is today, was British Waterways. The Number Ones used to try to get to a place before you and they used to throw you out on your loading, or your unloading. Anything to mess you up. That's why you didn't have friends, because everyone was for themselves and it was entirely up to them, but if they sent you from Birmingham and say they wanted you to go straight up through the night to get to a certain place to load up in the morning, they would only send the people they knowed would do it. I have knowed people to be in the office at Birmingham, the same time as meself and they've told them there'd been no loads back from Birmingham, and they'd send 'em to the coal pits, and the moment they'd gone through the first set of locks in Birmingham, they have told me the places to load from and they would tell you what time you have to be there to load up.'

Ted enjoyed working on the canals and the competition and sense of achievement when he reached his destination in record time. He also found that, in spite of all the rivalry, when the occasion arose the canal people would look after each other. At times it must have been quite difficult for a newcomer to get work on the canal boats.

'The very first person that gave me a pair of commercial boats, the bloke was called Ted Wood. He was a Grand Union Canal Carrying Company gaffer, before it was the British Waterways, so he knowed all

Ted enjoyed working on the canals.

the history about the canals and all the history about the families of the canals, so it was he who'd push you on. A lot of those gaffers what was in offices at Bull's Bridge was the people, at that time, that started me Dad and others off for Fellows, Morton and Clayton's, so when it was nationalized those gaffers swapped over to British Waterways. So, he knowed all the family well enough, you know . . .? There was two on us. There was two Ted Wards. The other one died anyhow, me uncle.'

Just as a man may become proud and even attached to his car, Ted was fond of his boats and seemed to enjoy repeating their names. 'My first boats that ever I had was a butty boat called *Capella* and a motor boat called *Bodner* and those were the very first two boats that ever I worked for meself. Well, in fact all my working life I only had two butty boats, one was the *Capella*. Yes, it's well knowed. I had two or three different motor boats. One called *Badsey* and one called *Centauria*, but the one butty, the *Capella*, stayed more or less all the way through.'

Ted and Bodmin.

Ted also had an early experience to tell, of working with a horse-drawn boat. 'I had one 'orse fall in. In fact, he didn't exactly fall in, I pushed him in because he wouldn't pull a blinking boat out the lock. We had this 'orse and he come from a firm in Birmingham called Ellimans and when it was brought over to Northampton locks it was so much of using its own route, it had his own ideas, this 'orse did, and it wouldn't pull a boat from the top of the flight of Northampton locks. I could understand it at the end, because the people who had the 'orse they used to pull the boat by hand at the first lock and let the 'orse do the work from the next lock down. Well, on this boat at the top of the Northampton locks, it wouldn't pull. It was just layin' in the line and wasn't doing a thing. But there again, I was young and I hadn't got patience for all this caper, so I pushed the 'orse in the cut and then I had to keep me head to get it back out. I had to lead it along the cut. I didn't gain a thing. It was just me temper at the time, but it was funny really, because I took it down the next lock, gets it out above the lock head and I hung it onto the line. I'd calmed down by the time I got back. I got a line, hung it onto the line and pulled the boat. And I got a bucket and scrubbed the 'orse down at the next lock to get all the mud off it. I didn't have any trouble with it after that and I'll tell you what, nobody else had any trouble with it. After then it didn't play up again. It just had strange ways. All 'orses do, funny enough.

'My father, in his early days, used to have an 'orse boat. He told me that the 'orses was so well trained for the canals that after they'd done the length you could loosen them off and they'd find their way back to the stable where they'd come from and you didn't have to walk behind them. If they had an 'orse that didn't pull itself unless somebody was walking behind it, they used to tie a boot behind it on the swingle-tree; that's a crossed piece of wood over his back, like a plough 'orse wears. Then the 'orse would find his own way. They would take a piece of rope

Horse-drawn boats at Ravensdale, Tunstall, Stoke-on-Trent.

and tie a boot on the other end of it, so the boot would drag the bottom while the 'orse was walking. They would do that to save walking behind the 'orse and the 'orse would think there was somebody behind it all the time. The 'orse would keep pulling the boat like anything perhaps for seven or eight miles. It's hard to believe, but when me dad had an 'orse boat, and also the wife's dad, they would know one another's 'orses by the sound of the feet going through the bridges. They would know the different sounds of their shoes, of the weights and everything, and they knowed who it was. I have 'eard me dad say this and when me wife's dad was alive, he said this as well.'

As time moved on, horses were exchanged for engines. National's were used in the British Waterway's boats and Bolinder's in those of Fellows, Morton and Clayton and Thomas Clayton, the tar boats. For a few decades the canals prospered until, slowly, loads became fewer and the competition fiercer. Now the competition was not between the canalmen themselves, but from a new source – the juggernaut. This became the 'King of the Road', stealing the commercial cargos once hauled by canal boats.

'I was the very last one to finish on commercial and that was for Willow Wren. I did the last run to a lot of different places. I finished twenty-three years ago. I knowed Willow Wren's were packing up, it was a dying trade. There was no money to be earned in it and you were just about plodding along and there was no future in it. I like canal work very much, don't get me wrong, but you have to consider your pocket more than anything. As Willow Wren said, they were coming to the end of carrying coal to John Dickinson's, they were going on to oil, and I was the last one. I decided to pack up meself and I took the last load of coal to John Dickinson's, Croxley Green. It was halfway through the summer when I finished. Just over twenty-two years ago.

'When British Waterways decided to pack up in 1963, a lot of people say it was to do with the frost, the 1962 to '63 frost, but it wasn't. I know for a fact it wasn't, but quite a few people didn't see it the same way. They done a lot of contract work. . . . The contracts was just about running out on a lot of the jobs. . . . Now I knowed it was going to happen this way, because I knowed that sooner or later British Waterways would finish the contracts and that was it. They were winding 'em up.'

Nevertheless, Ted recalls that some people continued to say it was the hard winters that caused the commercial canal traffic to cease operating, but although this was not Ted's opinion, he still remembers them well.

'It's only about three winters, in the years that I was in charge of boats, that I can say were bad winters. The hard one of 1962, right, that was thirteen weeks' hold up and I was working at Brentford, Middlesex. It froze that bad I broke the ice on the Thames and that was running water and the Thames froze up.

'British Waterways used to have loads of what they called ice-boats and you could break the ice up to ten inches, twelve inches thick, and after then, you can forget the idea. There would probably be eight or nine blokes in this ice-boat and they would be rocking this boat as the boat was going along. They would be rocking it to crack the sides as well as the front. So a boat would then go along and the others would follow it. They would have to follow it straight away. In that hard frost, the one we had just before I packed up, that was about fourteen to fifteen inches and it was thirteen weeks' hold up. My job for British Waterways then was using all the boats we could get hold on for storage boats, 'cos there wasn't enough room in the depots for the cargo. The yards were full of goods and they had to get as many boats as they could get 'old on for storage 'til winter was gone.

'I was on the boats, but so as I could be getting my wages every week, I had to go as a lock-keeper for the freeze-up. They had to keep

A horse-drawn iceboat, 1900. (National Waterways Museum)

the locks broke, so the lock side didn't push out with the ice and crack all the walls and everything. Tell you, it was a hard job that was. We had to keep the water running up and down the locks and that would keep the locks on the move and it didn't get time to freeze up round the locks, but that was going day and night and we had to.

'When I came to be finished with the commercial side of it, British Waterways said to me: "Do you want to leave or do you want to take one of our jobs on maintenance? If you leave you won't get no redundancy." So you had no choice but to take the next thing that come along. So that's how I come to do dredging in the first place. That involved cleaning the canals out, a couple or three mud-boats and a steam dredger; that was at Basingstoke. That was the system, but the money was so poor. It was even worse than the commercial days, because the commercial days, when I was on the waterways, there was no limit on it, 'cos the faster you worked the more you got, but when you come to be working for the maintenance, on the company, you was limited to how much hours you could work.

'It was to keep the canals clear and I found a body once around London. You would accidentally find them too. You would notify the police and probably go to Court and lose out at the end of the day, to the inquest. A lot of people used to get 'em out and put 'em back in again. You know, because it was too much trouble for the loss of earnings for the day. And the true ol' cockneys, they used to be on the tugs down London and I 'ave seen 'em pull many a one out and empty their pockets and push 'em back in. I was on the commercial at the time for the British Waterways and this tug there was raking this body out and I said, "What you got there? Ah, I suppose he's thrown himself in. What will you do, phone the police up?" "Ah, no," he said, "We'll throw him back in after we've taken the stuff out of 'is pockets." I can understand it, really,' reasoned Ted, nodding his head, 'because my mother and father, they got one out the canal at King's Langley, a body like, and they had to get back from Birmingham and it wasn't even worth the bother. They went from Birmingham by train to Hemel Hempstead and they never got paid properly, so you can see why people does it. It might be a bit different now, but in them days you didn't get money for doing what you were supposed to do.

'I can tell you another thing,' went on Ted, 'Commercial Road docks now, in Limehouse, in the days when I'm talking about, going back in the '60s like, well, the dock coppers were as bent as anyone else, because I've been in the docks and I've gone out of the gate at the night-time and they come and they be trying to sell me fags and bottles of whisky, and that's the dock coppers. All off ships or backs of lorries. I'd come to the gate and a security gate copper would say, "Do you want to buy some of this gear I've got here?" and that's security gate coppers. It used to go on everywhere, it used to go on.'

Ted also converted commercial boats to pleasure boats for a few years and believes it is good to keep the canals alive by using them for pleasure activities. However, he also feels that some people do not show sufficient care and respect when enjoying their leisure time on the canals and this, he thinks, is the cause of the rise in the rat population.

'Although canals are knowed for rats I don't think the boats would stop long enough to get a rat on! I tell you what they would do. They would go on [the boat] if you'd got grain on and we didn't have to get rid of them. They'd get rid of themselves when we unsheeted. They would be gone. As though they must have known the load was coming out. Well, I was at Wolverhampton going back a few years ago and Wolverhampton top lock was full of rats. They've made it into a leisure park and the fish and chip shop was just up the road from the bridge and people were dumping the paper and stuff on the canal side and the rats were having a field day. We stayed there for a while, but we moved on, there were too many, and that was in the daylight.

'There are more rats now with pleasure boats than there were in the earlier days, but just before we packed up there were getting more, because with the pleasure boats there was getting more litter on the side of the canals. Now you go through the canal at Leamington, or Birmingham, or around Paddington, they used to be a dumping ground, not from the boats, it was mostly from the houses and flats and that's when they started creeping in. They are having a big clean-up campaign at the moment, but it is overcrowded with rats now. I still say it's too much rubbish dumped on canals.'

When Ted is not off dredging he spends his time at home, painting canal-ware and making rope fenders for friends. Now his hobbies, these were once tasks he learned when on board his boat. 'Fender-making goes back for generations. You learn by watching other people and you just watch them and talk to them while they're doing them and you just pick it up from them. There ain't no skill to it at all. People buys the books now to learn how to do 'em, but we did not have to. Well, I buy the rope from here, in Coventry. There is a special sort of rope. You can buy the thick barge rope for inside the fenders, for what they call the packing, and you can buy the coarse sisal rope for casing them over. What you use is two sizes; about two inch for the middle, for casing, and go down to about an inch for tapering off. It makes them a neat finish like, but people does 'em with nylon rope, with bits of rope and all this and it's not a proper job.' Unfortunately, like most hobbies, it does not come cheap. 'You pay say, for 160 ft rope, up to £55 to £65 and ten years ago it would have been about £20. I can do mats and all sorts of knotted stuff.'

Ted is pleased to retain this special link with his old way of life, to introduce his land-bound friends to these unusual skills and prove to them that there is more to life on the cut than just plain haulage. 'Yes, my friends like the painted things and the knotted stuff.'

Chapter Four

A NARROW BOAT ARTIST

RONALD HOUGH

Ronald Hough

In the quietness of the Northamptonshire countryside sits the huge Braunston Marina. This enormous basin, formed from old reedy reservoirs, is now stuffed with craft of all kinds and all colours. There is an air of expectancy; brightly coloured pleasure boats are abundant and their owners tinker about with them, touching up paintwork, tying ropes and filling water-cans in readiness for their next journey. One or two forlorn old narrow boats which have seen better days of work and dirt, pride and achievement, float lazily on the water.

As well as smart new townhouses, along the wharf are several low buildings and sheds where a multitude of services for the fitting out of boats is offered: carpentry, upholstery, fender-making, painting and signwriting. Even if not participating in canal life, 'gongoozlers' (as visitors are called in canal-boat people's dialect) come to wander and browse, stand and stare. Canal-boat art, as it has become known, is an important ingredient in the magic of the canal; could it be the multi-coloured nature of these cheerful craft that attracts and arouses the curiosity of the constant flow of visitors?

Ronald painting a castle scene. (Coventry Evening Telegraph)

In the village of Braunston itself is the home of Ron Hough, an artist responsible for the decorative paintwork on many a canal boat. He decorates historic working boats converted to pleasure craft and especially those built in the old narrow boat style. Ron has seen many changes as freight traffic has moved away from the canals, but there has always been a hankering for the past and, of course, part of that is the traditional style of decorating canal boats: this still keeps Ron busy.

There have been long and lengthy discussions about when and why canal boats started to be painted decoratively and the origin of the particular motifs and scenes that were used. A comparison has been drawn between these boats and the tradition upheld by the Romany gypsies, who decorated their caravans in a similar way, but Ron is adamant that, 'the boatmen covered a lot of miles and painted what they saw, the castles at Chirk, Windsor and Warwick and the rambling roses along the hedgerows and perhaps a stream wending its way under a bridge. There's a lot more to it than "roses and castles", but a lot of people do try to look into it for a lot more than there really is! When I first worked we would put a swan, or a dog's head or a horse's head. Sometimes I have painted diamonds, clubs and hearts, but oh! I don't want spades painted on my boats. They are unlucky [as any fortune-teller will tell you].'

There is evidence that the tradition of canal-boat art goes back well over a century, to the time when the Empire was still expanding, so what better symbols to use than castles and roses, to brighten up the boats and the restricted cabins which were homes as well as workplaces for the boatmen and their families. Decorative painting was surely an ideal way to raise self-esteem.

Ron was born in Birmingham in 1934 and came to Braunston as a baby. He has lived there ever since, apart from his stint in the army on national service. 'I don't know what made me go into it,' Ron ponders, 'it was hard work really. Nobody else in my family had worked with the boats.' Some say it is a craft that can be taught but, without a doubt, nobody could turn out work as skilfully as Ron, unless they have some sort of artistic leaning. His first job was as an apprentice wood-machinist, but, unhappy with this as a potential career, he made a change and went to Samuel Barlow's boatyard. 'A lot of the working boatmen once owned their own boats, but when the motor boats came in most sold out to larger companies, like Samuel Barlow's and Fellows, Morton and Clayton. They were both carriers.' Samuel Barlow's eventually took over Nurser Brothers at the Braunston dockyard which was a long-standing company concerned with boat-building, maintenance and painting. Established in 1878 by William Nurser, the business was carried on by two of his sons, Charles, and Frank who concentrated on the painting work. Nurser's was a small firm and all the boat-builders were expected to be able to do a certain amount of good quality paintwork. Ron is a modest man and believes he had no special gift, just an appreciation of colour harmonies, but nevertheless, he was picked out as showing a particular ability and was apprenticed to Frank Nurser, who is said to have been one of the best canal-boat painters of his time. 'I learned to paint by watching Mr Nurser, Frank. When I worked with Frank you had to do it right, "If you are going to do it boy, do it right or don't do it at all."'

Over the years, the art of canal-boat painting has moved from the bargee to the artist in the boatyard and in the process has often become mechanical and stylized. Ron confirms that this trait did not affect Frank Nurser. 'He was a good artist and his boats could be picked out from all the others because his flowers came to life.'

Frank was meticulous in the execution of his paintings and Ron says that after a serious illness he became even more precise, as if to ensure the trade would continue to his high standards after he was gone. Frank died in 1952, but although his own work has become more and more difficult to find, he has left behind him men who have continued to paint

Ronald puts the finishing touches to a group of roses for Clevanda.

high-quality work of which he would have been proud. As Ron says, it is the names of the boats that have changed rather than the traditional motifs. Although he might be asked to do paintings to match more traditional boat names, such as *Thistle, Bramble, Harebell*, or perhaps *Lincolnshire Poacher*, today there is a preponderance of modern names. *Westminster Overdraft, Douganiris* and *Foxy Lady* are some recent requests.

When Ron first began his painting career, many of the boats were still working boats. 'In those days when you worked on a boatyard you had big hobnail boots so as any stray nails didn't go into your feet when you were walking about, because everywhere you went with wooden boats there was great big nails left in or sticking up. Not like today, you have steel boats and you have soft rubber boots.'

Boats that belonged to, or were on contract to, big companies had to be kept in particularly good order and were very well decorated. Ron remembered he used to paint the Ovaltine boats in the company colours, displaying their name and logo. In this way they could be easily picked out on the water and their name would be well advertised. 'I can remember one family, the Stokes's, and we used to paint their boats. They were spotless clean and when we were painting theirs, we had to go up with a pair of plimsolls to paint the roof. They couldn't have hobnail boots scratching the paint on their boats.'

The boats were usually brought into dry dock if there was extensive work to be done on them. 'We would float them into the dock, put the gates in, and then there is a panel in the end and the water runs away. In some docks they pump the water out, but there's not many like that, the sheds always seemed to have a free flow of water where they were built. It would go out the other end or there would be a huge pipe put in and the water would go off under the canal and down a brook or somewhere. 'Our shed was completely undercover, but some of them were just a roof; big open-sided sheds, and we had brazier fires in the winter. No, I can't work with gloves on. I've had my sister knit me some mittens and I can never wear them. I've got three or four pairs of mittens hanging about that I try with, but I can't get on with 'em. You just have to let your hands get cold.' He smiled, clapping his hands and rubbing them together, reliving the chill of those winter days.

Nevertheless, there are some events that Ron can look back upon and laugh at, even though they were not so funny at the time. 'One morning I was painting on the fore-end of the boat and for scaffolding we always used old boat planks. Boat planks that had the end broken off them, or been split, and they were all spiked together again. Well, I was on the fore-end and the damn thing broke and gave way, and I tips a load of white lead all over the floor. Frank was more interested in telling me off,

"What do you think about that paint, boy? The cost of that paint?" He was more interested in the paint than whether I had hurt myself or not.'

Times were different then; goods were still scarce in those post-war days and the pennies were carefully counted. 'We got paid on Friday night about a quarter of an hour before you came home, so you didn't get too excited about what you were going to do with your money! That was the last thing you got on Friday night. Payday.

'My first wage packet was £1 2s 6d a week and I used to take the half-crown back into the apprentices' department and they would give you a book of tickets. That was 11d return each one. So that was roughly half as much again as what the half-crown was worth, and because you were an apprentice you got these tickets, these five tickets to use on the bus to go to Braunston from Rugby, so that left you with £1 to bring home. They made sure they got you to work. There were 30d in a half crown, so you were gaining 25d, twenty-five old pennies a week.

Whether Ron is painting large boats or tiny souvenirs, he has his own three golden rules which he always follows: 'Use good-quality paint, good-quality brushes and know what you are doing. Not like some think, just a blob and then a bit here and a bit there. If you watch a craftsman at work, a good painter at work, well, it always looks easy, and you say, "Ooh, that looks easy, I can do that." All right, it is basically brushwork, but it's knowing how to do the brushwork, isn't it? And put it in like. It's a simple brush-stroke, but it is a question of putting things in the right place and blending the colours correctly. You know you can put colours that go right with one another, or they don't. They have got to harmonize and you have got to have an eye to do it really,' says Ron modestly. 'If you give somebody a boat to do and somebody else a similar boat and didn't let them see what one another were doing, one would come out quite pleasant to the eye and the other would not be marked out properly and would have spoiled the job.'

Ron usually starts his work by marking out the design. He paints in the hearts of the flowers with dark paint, then puts the first application of paint on the leaves, to give the basic shape and placement of the final design. He then builds upon this, 'Yes, you've got to blend the colour in so you get the centre of the rose.' He then completes the roses, adding stamens and a sprinkling of daisies of various sizes. 'Sometimes, it is all according to what the background is, sometimes, you make a very dark centre and pull out around the light colours and another time, if you want to highlight it a bit more, you put your lighter colours in the middle and just a little bit of dark around the outside. I don't use much red. Basically, you work from dark to light which looks quite nice, because you get the highlights round the outside then. The colour of the boat will decide if you use a dark or a light design. If it is in the fore-end, in the well where it's dark, you would do a light centre so as to lift it a bit.'

Ron believes a lot of the skill is in the marking out and sometimes, 'I have had one or two awkward customers. I've just had one: "I've seen this on that boat, and I want this." So I said, "Well, all right, it looks right on that boat, but it won't look right where you want it, round that porthole, because there en't enough room for it." I mean, they will come along with a picture and they'll say, "Oh, I want this in that space, or I want B.J. and R.A. SIMPSON and SONS", and they've got a small panel at the back and there's no way you are going to get it in. Instead of say, B. and R. SIMPSON or THE SIMPSON FAMILY, or something like this, which would be better, they want every initial and you have to convince them that it's not going to look right. But most see what work I've done and they just leave it to me to set it out right and balance it right and put it in right.'

It is the habit of many canal-boat artists to use a maul stick. This is a short stick held with the left hand so the right hand, the painting hand, can rest upon it, but Ron does not usually find this necessary. 'Signwriters use a maul stick and if you start off with a maul stick, I suppose it's quite handy to do it, but we never did. Now, if you are painting roses you don't want a maul stick to paint a rose, or to paint a picture, you do that freehand, so in the meantime you do your writing exactly the same. I do sometimes just hold one hand on the other, hold me right hand on top of me left, but if I'm doing a rose and castle, I don't. With lettering I might, just to steady it a bit.'

Ron has a great sense of humour and when asked what makes his painting stand out from that of other people, he filled the room with a huge roar of laughter. 'It's better!' he claimed jovially. Yet he still retained his modesty and went on more seriously: 'When I paint castles, people can tell they are mine. Mine have a distinctive shape. The patterns are handed down, plus the fact that you add a few more designs. The thing is knowing how to build it up, I suppose, and to paint it quick. Paint the background and build your castle up, so as it's got a bit of depth to it, but if some people just copy, they don't get it right, do they?'

Although Ron has his own ideas about design, he is wary of current fashions and he is very considerate towards the ideas of the people he is working for. 'You have to keep them basically to what the boat will take and what the people want. Some people want a plain one and some people will want quite a lot of work on it. Scrolls have come into fashion quite a lot more in this area. Scrolls used to be more of a northern pattern on boats, but they are all over the place now. The other thing you see now is the fish. It's a religious symbol and it's only a few strokes. Well, now you see that on some of the boats sometimes. There are quite a lot of religious cult groups locally.'

Since the 1960s, Ron has been freelancing and has continued painting boats and some of the furnishing and items for the cabins. 'A boat, a real

Ronald at work in his studio. Canal art has become popular as giftware.

narrow boat, not the hire boats, has two watercans, a three gallon one and a two gallon one, and they would keep fresh water all the while. Some folk would have their name on them, and some of them wouldn't. They would have a handbowl and they always have a stool and sometimes a tray of their own. It's only pleasure boats that have a plant bowl on top; that would get knocked off on a working boat.'

Ron went on to explain how he painted mop handles, making it sound extremely simple. 'Yes, oh yes, I do those like barber's poles,' he grinned knowingly. 'I set it out with a piece of cotton. Say you got your pole, and say that was four foot long, you perhaps mark it into four lots of twelve inches. You fix a piece of cotton on the top and wrap it round the pole, hitting each mark. Then you just follow the first one round in white, put the yellow in between and then, when you took your cotton off, it would leave you a sharp line. Then, when the white and yellow is dry, you then cut the red and blue into the white by hand, twisting it as you go round; so it will be red, white, blue and yellow. You put a nail in one end to hold it with and twist the pole. Or, you could put a hook in, so you could hang it up. The tiller of the boat is done in the same way.'

Once Ron did a spell of painting quality giftware for firms like Heals and we were delighted to discover that an ornamental watering-can I had bought from Heals, way back in the 1960s, is one that Ron had painted!

There was a time when Ron thought the canals would die completely, but by the time working narrow boats ceased to operate, the leisure industry had taken over and Braunston Marina continued to thrive and become a leading centre for canal boating. Samuel Barlow's boats were among those to be converted to pleasure boats. The tradition of canal-boat painting lives on too, but Ron has a secret smile about some of the changes: 'The British Waterways came along and all you got was blue and yellow boats, then they brought transfers in!' Ron found this very amusing. 'They used to have transfers of roses and castles on the back. They used to paint the boats blue and yellow and put transfers of roses and castles on the doors. Yes, British Waterways, they were the culprits. There are a few about now, but they don't last, the transfer doesn't last on the boat that long, it comes off when it's outside. It's all right if it's on a door and it's going to be shut, so that it's inside as much as it's out and not in the weather all the while. But these transfers that they put on, they peel off in the weather.'

It will be a sad day if the traditional art of canal-boat painting disappears but Ron can be justly proud when he says: 'Ours were always painted on.'

NURSES ON THE 'CUT'

Nurse Carrina Rutter

There was little in the way of medical attention for those who lived and worked on the 'cut' and even when treatment was available follow-up care was frequently difficult to obtain due to the boat people's nomadic existence and a reluctance to seek help from the unknown. To help overcome this problem, some philanthropic bodies set up clinics and surgeries. The Medical Mission, a religious organization, opened a clinic near the canal wharves in Birmingham and, in association with the Birmingham General Hospital, this was still open in 1944. There was a subscription of a few pence a week, or a fee to cover treatment, but for those who worked for Fellows, Morton and Clayton, there were fewer worries; the company paid a corporate annual subscription and in return nurses would go out to the boats to attend confinements.

After the Public Health Act of 1907, those children who were lucky enough to go to school had the advantage of seeing one of the nurses who made frequent visits. Although commonly known as 'Nitty Norah', the nurse would also look out for any other health problems and treat minor ills and injuries. The most popular and well-loved carers along the waterways seem to have been those who worked voluntarily out of sheer kindness. One such lady was Sister Mary Ward. Although said to be unqualified, she had gained some experience of nursing. When she went to stay at Stoke Bruerne to care for her ageing father, her sympathy was moved by the plight of the canal-boat people and she converted a room of her lock-side cottage into a surgery, providing free treatment for them. One old boatwoman says, 'She was our doctor and our nurse. If we had anything wrong we would always run to her and she would know what to do with us.' Although her services were provided free of charge, all the funding Sister Mary received was £2 per week from the Grand Union Canal Carrying Company.

It could not have been easy to work in the front room of the little cottage where there was no gas, electricity or telephone and even water had to be brought from the village well, but Sister Mary Ward was happy to help in return for the love she received from her grateful patients. In 1951 she was awarded the OBE in recognition of her services and was presented with a traditionally painted Buckby water can by the appreciative canal-boat people.

When she was a child, Carrina Rutter lived close to the canal in Nuneaton and went to the local school. 'When I was at school, we had one little boy come to the school from a boat, but he wasn't put in the classroom with the other children. He was only seen at assembly in the morning and after the hymns were sung he was off and we never saw him again until it was time to go home, but everybody was curious. Even though we lived near the canal, you didn't see very many boat children. We did not know what happened to him. Perhaps he was taken off for extra attention because he was behind. He didn't seem very happy. Everybody was envious because he lived on a boat and he didn't come to school very often. In fact, I don't think he ever came again.'

Many years later when Carrina grew up, she became a nurse at what was once known as Nuneaton Cottage Hospital. 'It was the Nuneaton Cottage Hospital originally, but when I worked there from 1968, it had become part of the Coventry and Warwick Group 8 Hospitals.

'The women from the canals did not usually come in to have their babies, they usually had them on the boats. They tended to find a doctor or a midwife that they knew and trusted and go to where they were and sort of plan the birth to be in that area.'

It must have been difficult for the mother and the nurse delivering a baby in such a restricted space. There was no running water and the other children of the family might have to play outside or stay with somebody from another boat if there was one nearby, but the boat people were always willing to help one another on such occasions.

Women and children on Golden Spray. *(National Waterways Museum)*

'We had canal-boat children come into the hospital occasionally and we had special rules for them. If any child who was a gipsy, traveller or a boat child came into the Accident and Emergency Department, they had to be "de-nitted" before they were sent up to the wards and it did not matter how ill they were, they were not allowed into a hospital bed until their head had been de-liced. The only case that I had to deal with, the child had asthma and was very distressed and the mother was with it and was distressed also, but we still had to do it with a nit comb, a really antiquated procedure. They did have to be bathed as well, but because they were boat children they were assumed to be lousy. This child wasn't, but it did not matter how much the mother protested that the child was clean. Originally the rules applied to adults as well, but by the time I was there, I think that they had had some protestations from the adults and the staff were no longer prepared to hold them down to do it.

'At the small hospital in Nuneaton there wasn't a children's ward as such, so they went on to an ordinary ward. They had to go into the bed next to the sister's office where usually the most ill patients were put, but if they were a traveller, or a boat person, they had to go into that bed so that the sister and the nurses could keep an eye on them.

'This particular child that was de-nitted was about seven and she was only in for a couple of days. Because they were travelling, apparently it wasn't easy for them to get to a doctor to get a prescription and so she had run out of medication. She knew she was asthmatic and the mother knew what medication she needed, but they had just run out. She had an attack unexpectedly and this particular child stayed for two days in the general women's ward and at the end of the two days, when the mother came to collect her, both the mother and the child went round each bed shaking hands and saying goodbye, which I have never seen before.

'The little girl was clean, very clean, and the mother and father and a little brother came to visit the child usually. Apparently in the past, if a member of the family was in the hospital, the parents and relations were quite reluctant to visit. I think this was probably because the sisters looked down on them and sort of wanted them to wash their hands and so on before they went in.

'This child's clothes were quite ordinary, but I remember when I was very small, my grandfather lived overlooking the canal, and the canal-boat children always looked ragged, but their underclothes, when you got to see them, always seemed very clean. And they were embroidered. It was as if they couldn't take pride in their outer garments, but they did in the inner ones that nobody saw except themselves. When the little girl lifted her dress to be examined, she had pretty pantaloons. They were sort of old-fashioned dressed, were the children that we saw.

'Other nurses that had been at the hospital a long time, remembered having to do the same de-nitting procedure to the adults and that wasn't always well received, but one nurse told me, she had been there twenty years and of all the canal and gipsy children whose hair she had had to go through, she had never found anything there. So how long it had been going on, I don't know, or whether it is now. I left in 1972.'

Chapter Five

CLASSES ON THE 'CUT'

LEONARD BALL

Leonard Ball

Leonard Ball once worked for Cadbury's and lived in Bournville before his retirement. Some of the most vivid memories of his working life are of his early experiences on the canals and later working at 'Waterside', Cadbury's canal-side wharf. 'Canals were once part of the Cadbury way of life. One of the reasons why Cadbury's built the Bournville factory at that site was because it was close to the canal and the railway. That was their mode of transport for doing things, plus horse and cart. The Company had used the canals right from its earliest days and it was not until the 1960s that it actually stopped using them to carry products between various factories. It wasn't just the cheapest method of transport, it was also the "greenest".' This was an ideal valued by Cadbury's long before the modern concern for the environment became the norm.

It was expected that when Leonard Ball reached fourteen he would go to work for Cadbury's. It was the 'done thing' in those days for the children of Cadbury staff to follow in their parent's footsteps and 'get in at the chocolate factory'. So in April 1943, Leonard started work at the

Cadbury's 'camp school on a barge'. (Cadbury Limited)

Bournville factory where, like his father before him, he eventually became an engineer. It was through Cadbury's educational programme for their young employees, however, that Leonard got to know the canals and he looks back with keenness, not to say affection, on those summer days of his youth and the camaraderie of the other lads when they went off on their adventures aboard a narrow boat. "Camp school on a barge", as it was called, was a journey lasting about a week, travelling along the canals by narrow boat. So, over a number of weeks, perhaps 200 to 250 teenage boys from the Company would have an opportunity to do this trip. Each year the trip changed to a new destination. The ones I took part in were in 1946, when I went to Worcester and Tewkesbury, 1947, to Market Drayton, Nantwich and Chester and in 1948, Warwick, Braunston and Northampton. Those are the trips that I did, but these trips had been in operation long before that, starting in 1917.'

It is no longer unusual to find children on canal boats or in groups on the tow-path, working on school projects concerning the canals and learning about their natural history along the way, but when Cadbury's started their 'school on the barge', they were pioneers in the field. In the early years they had owned several canal boats and *Bournville No. 6* was used to take three groups of boys, over a period of three weeks, from the wharf at Bournville to Bishopton, near Stratford-upon-Avon. They were given the opportunity to study natural history, make factory visits and excursions to various towns and cities of historic interest *en route* and to experience the way of life on a working boat. The first trip set a pattern that was to be followed for over forty years.

'For forty-eight weeks of the year the narrow boat was a working boat carrying materials, but it was taken out of service for the school camp. At the wharf area known as Waterside the carpentry department prepared a covering that was fixed to convert part of the boat into an enclosed classroom for the camp school barge. This upper structure was stored when the boat was working, and brought out and used again year after year for the camp school.'

Competition for places was always very keen. 'A holiday with paid leave of absence!' could only be met with enthusiasm. However, only those with good reports from the 'Day Continuation School', which they were obliged to attend one day a week, could apply to take part in the expedition.

'I'm a hoarder,' says Leonard sentimentally and he still treasures his three diaries, one made each year on his canal trips. They are a faded and memorable record, carefully written in his boyish hand, of those carefree days of youth. One never to be forgotten memory was a visit to the salt mine at Crewe. 'During the war a million pounds' worth of mercury was stored there, together with many other things of fabulous value.' Leonard still remembers the harsh working conditions in the factory and the hard labour carried out by the men outside who loaded the huge rough blocks of salt by hand on to the boats – which carried 11 tons when fully laden – to be transported to Gas Street Basin, Birmingham, where they were cut up and sold to shops and factories.

Apart from these excursions there were other important things to do. 'We were allocated duties in the mornings, so it was Joe's job to clean the boat; Fred's job to feed and water the horse; Henry's job was to look after the horse going along the tow-path and to make sure all was well, but the overall running of the boat, as far as the canal was concerned, was that of our No. 1 (Mr and Mrs Ballinger to us, but Chocolate Charlie and Olive to their mates). They were working people, working bargees. For the rest of the year they were part of the organization that brought goods to the Company. The Ballinger Company had been going for some time.

'When we came to the locks, like on the Worcester Canal, where there are nearly thirty locks all the way from King's Norton down to the River Severn, it was our job to open and close them under the supervision of Mr Ballinger, and that really was hard work. Along the way we still had to find various plants or look for various buildings or point out milestones in the building of the canals. There are some very interesting buildings, still to this day. There's a pumping station for pumping water from one lock to another, where the flow isn't satisfactory due to gravity. All these things we were asked to look at and answer questions.'

When the camp school first started, the narrow boat was pulled by two donkeys, but by the time Leonard took part, 'the camp school barge was normally pulled by a horse, either Jack or faithful old Dolly, and one of the things we had to do was to lead the horse along the tow-path.' Near Nantwich, the Welsh Canal joins the main 'Shroppie Cut', the name given to the canal that wends its way through Whitchurch to Llangollen and Welshpool. This stretch was no longer used at that time and green weed covered most of the water's surface, but full of adventure and high spirits the group chanced their luck and risked the trip to Whitchurch. 'We dragged along the bottom, we stuck on mud-banks and we jammed locks,' but Mr Ballinger knew all the tricks of the trade and cleverly persuaded the boat out of impossible situations. This caused great excitement and the boys' only grumble was that they had to walk the tow-path more than usual as the boat's load had to be lightened.

Another adventure happened along the Grand Union Canal, between Blisworth and Northampton. People gasped with amazement when they saw a horse-drawn boat on this route which hadn't had horses along its tow-path for many years. Heads shook, voices muttered, but the boys ventured forward in spite of the bush thickets, and brambles blocking the way and Leonard wrote in his diary: 'Had some fun getting round some very sharp bends and this meant a couple of tow-ropes and some hard work for Dolly.'

If there was a tunnel, the horse would be unhitched and hitched up again at the other end, but for the boys it was a different matter. 'When going through tunnels, as for instance going to Worcester, we had to go through the one-and-a-quarter mile long Tardebigge Tunnel and we helped Mr Ballinger with the "legging" as it was called. We were shown how to do this. So, laying on our backs on the top of the barge we walked along the sides or the top of the tunnel to keep the barge moving forward.' It inched forward at a snail's pace, moving sluggishly through the pitch darkness towards the pinpoint of light marking the end of the tunnel. 'Of course, we were noting the ruts that were made by the thousands and thousands of feet that had walked along the roof and the walls before us. It was a bit wet, slimy and messy, because the tunnels leaked. And they had stalactites hanging down. It was slippery and we were told to be careful. We enjoyed ourselves, it made us feel strong and important because we knew we were doing just what the old bargees had had to do. Just a few of the families still had their horses and would still do this legging, but the majority had motorized so it was not necessary.

'When we came to the bridges it was always a miracle as to how the horse could get underneath! It reminds me of one of the Black Country jokes where Enoch and Eli were looking at the horse and looking at the bridge and saying, "Ay, Enoch, the horse won't go under there 'cos it's too high. It ain't 'igh enough." So Eli says, "Well, 'ang on a bit, we'll dig a hole along the tow-path and he'll get through there then." An' Enoch says, "Don't be so daft, it ain't 'is feet that won't go under, it's 'is 'ead." So that sort of humour became part of our way of life as well.'

As Quakers and pacifists, Leonard remembers Cadbury's were selective about their part in the war effort but, 'They made respirators, five million of them, for the soldiers in the various armed forces. Those

'Legging' through Barnton Tunnel in 1960. (National Waterways Museum)

gas masks were packed in big containers and the containers were taken to the Waterside where they were loaded into the canal barges for removal to wherever they were required. So even in the war years the barges were used extensively to move the goods that we made. They were mostly non-belligerent things like jerry-cans, mangles; portable mangles for wringing clothes out. A whole range of pacifist-type goods, but they did make component parts and fittings for a dozen or more different types of aircraft, including Spitfires. On 3 December 1940, there was an air raid lasting thirteen hours and an enemy bomb fell at Bournville. It was disastrous. It pierced the aqueduct which carried the canal over Bournville Lane, next to the railway station. The lower floors of the factory were flooded and so were the houses and streets beyond the factory, but the canal was left empty!

Destruction caused in 1940 by an enemy bomb piercing the aquaduct carrying the canal over Bournville Lane. (Cadbury Limited)

'The maintenance of all the unloading area around Waterside was part of my responsibilities, along with other people like the carpenter and builders looking after the wharves and sides of the canal. On Waterside there were several warehouses used for storage and it was a hive of activity here during the days of unloading; coal, bags of crumb [a raw milk chocolate], milk itself, cocoa beans, sugar and engineering products that were needed for maintenance work, were transported from the Black Country where they were made. Coal for the power station came from the mine at Cannock Chase by barge, then that was unloaded and stockpiled at Bournville ready to burn in the boilers. The

Cadbury canal boats at Waterside, laden with churns of milk. The horse is grazing along the bank. (Cadbury Limited)

canals were used a lot by the organization for that sort of work, to carry things to the factory and from the factory.

'The canals were vital to the running of the chocolate factory. When they found out how to make chocolate, they realized they had to have a lot of milk and milk did not come from Birmingham, it comes from the countryside. So the company had to build factories in the countryside at places like Knighton and Bangor. The milk was collected from the farms and taken in churns on the narrow boats, to these factories and mixed with a liquor made from cocoa beans to make raw chocolate or "crumb". That was put into hessian sacks and loaded on to the canal narrow boats and taken to Bournville where it was made into dairy milk chocolate. Today, perhaps a dozen people do the whole job, where it perhaps took a hundred people to do it before.'

Chapter Six

LAST BOAT WITH CHINA

JAMES MORGAN, WILLIAM WILSHAW AND KENNETH BRAMMER

Jim Morgan

It is now a desolate wasteland, the stretch of the Caldon Canal that threads its way through the deserted factories and old kilns of the Potteries. A warm sunny day in spring should herald a new beginning, but the canal is becoming lifeless, signalling the end of an era. Most of the kilns have gone or have become museum relics; the factories are empty and idle and the silence is threatening. Johnson Brothers has closed down completely; the last pottery to use the Caldon to carry chinaware. Only pleasure boats will pass through now, not stopping, just getting through this dingy, sad stretch of water as quickly as possible.

Jim Morgan remembers earlier days when the Potteries were alive and throbbing with activity. The narrow boats came and went, even jostled for a place to put down and load up. 'The canals were really full in those days. No pleasure boats, they hadn't been thought of. It was a working area. The canal was a working area.'

Water was vital to the pottery industry, particularly as a means of transport, so it is not surprising that in 1779 the young entrepreneur Josiah Wedgwood promoted the building of canals through the Potteries. Needless to say, it was his potters, and those of the numerous other factories lining the banks of those canals, that provided most of the cargo. 'There is a little pub on the canal down at Stone, The Star, and it is reckoned that in that pub, it's still there, is where James Brindley and Josiah Wedgwood signed the contract, or whatever, to build these canals and that is why a lot of the potbanks [potteries] are very near to the canals. It was a good form of transport. Cheap and safe. They reckon it saved a terrific amount of breakages because the journey was so smooth.'

Jim grew up in the shadow of the kilns and his mother worked in the Potteries. Nowadays, being a very cheerful character and fond of a laugh, Jim makes light of his mother's job. 'My mother worked in the pots. She was what we called a "sticka-uppa". Now then, what's that? A sticka-uppa? The proper name is fettler – fettling the ware. You know, when you used to have the old-fashioned chambers in bedrooms? She were in the department that made them and she stuck the handles on. I was only a little one then, but I used to go on the bank to her, but you see in those sort of days there was a lot more freedom. You could walk on a potbank, there was no security or anything like that, especially if you had got someone working on there. You could go straight on the potbank to that person, to that person whoever it might be. That's how I used to go and see me mother from school. That's what she did. There was about 30,000 people in the Potteries in those days and all the ware was transported by canal boat. She worked on one in Stoke, but I went to Johnson's.'

When he was a youngster the tow-path was Jim's playground. The pleasures and entertainments of the canal were free and, along with the

other local lads, Jim often got into mischief. 'I used to live by the canal.
I used to live up there and we used to go along the canal doing damage
as kids. Digging our feet in the tow-path, picking up lumps of brick and
throwing them, and skimming stones across the water. Ducks and
drakes we called it. But they were simple, happy days. Nobody had got
any money and we never got into serious trouble. We swam in the canal.
I went in once and scored all me legs skimming the bottom. Shhhwip.
It's something you shouldn't have done, it wasn't clean. It was that area
down there by Shirley's Bone Mill. It was our happy hunting ground in
those days.' Some of the fun may have seemed like a joke, but many a
boatman would have cheerfully wrung their young necks if they had got
hold of those little devils.

'There was always a lot of boats moored up on the canal in those days
and what we used to do was play tricks on the boat people, which again
you shouldn't have done. We used to loose the boats off. Unhook the
ropes off the boats they used to fasten them, and give the boat a bit of a
push and it would go across other side of the canal. Not along the canal,
just drift across to the other side, you see. So, when the boatee came out
the pub, he'd got to walk a mile round to get to his boat and we used to
watch him. Because there was no tow-path on the other side, you see,
he'd have to go over the bridge, all the way round streets to get back to
the spare ground to get his boat again and bring it back to where we'd
took it off. Sometimes we got caught, so we'd run like mad along the
canal. The boatees, they were just passing through, we never got to
know them.'

This fun ceased when Jim was fourteen years old. In 1937 a lad was
considered old enough to earn his own living when he reached
fourteen, so he started work at Johnson Brothers. It was not a matter of
following in his mother's footsteps. 'It was just a matter of getting a job.
I knew someone that worked there and they got me a job and I finished

up round there. I was a packer before I became a loader and it was hard work, up and down steps with arms full of 'ware.'

Jim was glad when the opportunity came his way to become a loader. 'My first wage packet was 12s 6d and for loading the boat we used to get 6d an hour. Eh, and I might say, you used to run after that. Well, if you got a boat for the afternoon, you knew you were going to get 6d an hour for two or three hours' work. We took it in turns. There were about eight or ten of us in this packing house and we used to take it in turns to share the work out. You'd stop doing your job for the afternoon and go on to loading. You'd be stopped your usual money and get 6d an hour for loading the boat.

'I loaded narrow boats with 'ware. I might load one each day. One would come up loaded with flints. Druckles we called 'em. They came from Cornwall and they came all the way by canal and the boats were mostly horse-drawn. They were beginning to introduce the motor boat, but they were mostly horse-drawn. The druckles were unloaded, perhaps 20 or 30 ton of them, and then round about dinnertime the boat would be moved up here and we would fill it up with crates of 'ware to go up to Liverpool or wherever, for putting on ships. There was one packer fetching crates to what we called the boathole [the door from the pottery on to the canal bank]. We'd lower the crane's chain down and he'd put the hooks on the crate. We would line it up, swing it out to the boat, the boatee would be in the boat and he'd position it where he wanted it on the boat. Two layers. One layer on the bottom and one layer on the top. They couldn't go too high because of the low bridges in places. There were a couple of tunnels too. They had to unhitch the horse and he would be taken over the top and wait at Boathorse Lane while they legged the boat through. Eventually they had the first electrically driven boat and the tunnel-keeper used to wait 'til three or four barges came along and take two, three or four through at a time, but legging it through. That must have been hard work.

Johnson Brothers, Lichfield Street, Hanley.

'They [Johnson Brothers] used all different canal companies, Fellows & Co., Anderton & Co. We called the Anderton boats "knobsticks" and their crew were called "knobstick men". We were working away one day at boat'ole and there was a commotion on the canal side. A horse had fallen in canal. He was pulling the boat and he must have skidded backwards. Plop! In the water he went. The water was about 4 ft. The horse was in the water up to his body. The length of his legs, like. Well, it was all right. They unhooked him of his reins while we got him out. Well, we swung the crane out and the boatee put a harness round the horse and we pulled him up. Well, anyway, after a bit of a rub down and a bit of quietening down like, the horse, they attached him to the boat harness again and away they went! It was all over in a few minutes. They were happy days, you know.'

The war interrupted Jim's career at Johnson's and he was unable to return when the war finished. Johnson Brothers continued to transport raw materials and chinaware by barge, however, it was not long before it ceased to transport cargo over long distances by hired barge and a change was made to carry chinaware locally on its own barges. No longer were the various stages of manufacture carried out in one building, but in various departments in factories scattered along the Caldon. It remained practical for the chinaware to be transported from factory to factory by water.

Billy Willshaw

Billy Wilshaw started to work with Johnson Brothers in 1956 and he has been witness to the gradual decline in its use of the Caldon Canal; the last firm in the country to transport chinaware by water. He started to work the barges in the 1970s and stayed working on the canal until May 1995, when the last of Johnson Brothers's factories along the canal closed down and its chinaware ceased to be transported by boat.

April, 1995

'When I first started work on the barges I used to go to the Milton factory. It was about five miles from here and that closed down about ten years ago. Then we did what you called biscuitware. That's 'ware before it's decorated. We transported it from factory to factory. The factory at Eastwood, we used to supply them with 'ware off three factories and they used to decorate it and finish it and then we used to collect it and take it

Ken Brammer

down to the packing department.' Standing outside the pottery on the canal bank, Billy enthusiastically discusses the old barges with his colleague Ken Brammer, who started with Johnson Brothers in 1953. They have had many mutual experiences, working with the boats together, and talk animatedly, often sharing the storytelling. 'We used to have three boats, two were low boats,' says Billy, 'and two boatmen. They would do three loads each a day, or sometimes two, but of course, nowadays, we only have to go half a mile or so down the canal to Eagle Pottery. It's all going to move to Eagle Pottery where it's packed and we won't need a boat at all then. Well, it's only ten minutes, or sometimes it's longer if the wind's against you. Now we use what we call the catamaran.

'This boat, the catamaran, *Milton Maid* was designed by one of our engineers,' explains Ken. 'He was named Geoff Bird. Dicky Bird we used to call him, and he was the Chief Engineer. He designed it and the engineers built it. It's quite unique. You won't see anything like that again. It's made of steel; not a lot of maintenance.'

'So, now and again we have it out and paint it Wedgwood blue,' adds Billy. 'We're part of Wedgwood now.'

'The engine is a Morris 1000 engine, a car engine, and it just drives the propeller. You can see the propeller in the water, and it just goes along gently . . .'

'. . . approximately 4 mile an hour,' interrupts Billy, 'that's the speed you should go on a canal, no faster than that. That's the law, walking pace.'

The Johnson's catamaran, Milton Maid, *had a Morris 1000 engine. It is 60 ft long, 7 ft wide and carried about 5–6 tons.*

'Yes, it's done its share of work,' says Ken loyally. 'It's been a good one. It has been in use about twenty-seven years. It was the first one we had. One has gone and the other one is just up the road. They had that one first and they thought it was so good, it did that much work, they thought they would have another one. And they had another one after that. They used to use the two big low boats when they did the Milton run because that was a greater distance and they were a lot faster than this.'

'They'd got bigger engines,' joined in Billy, 'could take more weight. As soon as Milton shut, that was about 1984, they just used the catamaran.'

'Years ago when we used to go to Milton,' remembered Ken, 'we used to go forwards all the time because at Milton, there is a place just beyond, where it is wide enough for us to turn the boat round, but we don't bother now with *Milton Maid*. When we go to Eagle Pottery we just go forward and then reverse back. One chap, an engineer, he's retired now, he said, "It will do it no good, you know, reversing the boat over that distance." So I said, "Well, where do I turn it round?" "What do you mean?" "Well," I said, "the boat is 60 ft long and the canal is 10 ft wide. The only other way I could do it would be to go right to Milton which would probably be another forty minutes and come back again, that's another forty minutes, so it's an hour and a half you would be wasting." "Oh, I see what you mean," came the reply.

'Yes, this boat is 60 ft long and 7 ft wide and when we are fully loaded we get 5 or 6 ton on it, which is a good load.'

The two men talk of the boats as if they were old friends and their experiences, good or bad, are now looked upon as golden memories; never-to-be-forgotten episodes to be lingered over. Some incidents may have caused grief at the time, but because they had overcome these difficulties together, they now enjoy looking back at them with good humour and a smile.

There was one accident that was considered very annoying at the time, but it is now remembered by Billy with amusement. 'Once we lost some pottery in the canal. This boat that we have now, when we first had it, it flipped over. When they were loading it, they must have loaded it up a bit wrong and across at Hanley bank it flipped over. Nobody got hurt, but it went right over, it turned turtle. They must have been loading it wrong, you know, more on one side. We had all the 'ware go into the canal and we had divers down. People to get it up. What happened years ago, this factory took over the factory next door. They knocked holes in the wall to make it one big factory and at the time of the boat tipping over, there it was, all dirty and muddy and so all the 'ware was brought on to the cleaner part because we had plenty of room. So we got hosepipes and we were just washing it down like, like you do your cars. We reclaimed all of it. All that we could see, but this is a lot better than roads, eh Ken?'

'Yeah, just imagine roads. Somebody puts a foot on the brake, you've got to stop all of a sudden. Or turning a corner, or over bumps, or something like that. It has proved over many years that this is a much safer way of transporting crockery and we've got stabilizers now. It's certainly a lot cheaper.

'We've got another catamaran that we don't use anymore. This one actually floats on top of the water, but the other one, when it's loaded, it drops right down. It all depends on the water level as well,' explained Ken. 'Yes,' agreed Billy, 'because if the water level is down, we can't put much on. It doesn't depend on the weather or anything like that. A few years ago, we came in one morning, looked out on the canal, "Where's it gone?" One of the canal banks had collapsed and all the water was in the field. Yes, British Waterways, they look after the walls, they had been working on the banks along near Milton and where they'd been digging, the bank had just gone and all the water went out and all you could see was mud. The water had disappeared.' And that wasn't the end of the story. 'We usually tie the boat to the wall. We've got chains and two big locks on it and as the canal water went down, the barge was left hanging on to the wall.'

Unlike rivers, which flow from a natural source, canals have to be artificially fed with water. When the canals were privately owned, the canal owners were very jealous of their own canal-water supplies and went to great lengths to safeguard them. However, although catastrophies do still happen, it is no longer because one canal company is stealing another's supply of water.

Ken was eager to recount a recent event that could have resulted in total disaster. 'About three weeks ago, I came on about half past six or seven o'clock on the Monday morning; I looked across and I thought, what the heck's wrong with that boat? I could see something sticking up. It was a 5-inch gas pipe. We'd had vandals along the canal on Thursday. The water had gone out. They had breached the bank somewhere. Well, we rang the Waterways up, this was on Thursday, they said, "Well by Monday you might be back to normal," but on Saturday, at five o'clock, the police had called the engineer out. The barge was floating down the canal at Hanley Park, which is about a quarter of a mile away by Hanley Bridge. What had happened, the canal level had gone down due to vandalism of the bank, and the barge, being tied to the wall, had pulled the wall away and the wall had gone into the water. A lot of the banks are made up of pottery waste. They just used to bung it down the sides years ago. It was about 60 ft of wall that it had pulled down. If that gas pipe had been punctured we would have been in trouble because there are cars going over the bridge all the time and you've only to have a bit of gas and a spark. Well, we were lucky really. We did fetch the boat back in to sort the gas out, which they did, then that was the end of that as far as we know and just this last week they put the wall back just up there.'

'Of course, the kids sometimes cause water shortages,' Billy joined in jovially. 'There's locks at the bottom, down at Etruria way, and you know if you go two or three mile along, well, there's locks down there and if the children get messing with the locks, especially in the light nights, they leave the locks open and then when we come in, in the morning, half the water's gone. It's gone down you see, it just keeps going. Then we have to phone in and they let some more in from the reservoir, Rudyard Lake. That's where the canal is fed from. It's a great lake.' It is said that Mr and Mrs Kipling visited this lake and were so impressed with it that they chose the name Rudyard for their son, who was born soon after.

Most of the time Billy enjoys working in the open air, but admits it is not so pleasant in the harsh winter months when the canal might freeze and a biting wind whistles through the funnel created by the factories, which stand either side along the banks of the canal. Jim Morgan had talked of a time when 'winters were real winters' and it was possible to walk for miles along on the ice. 'It was not as it is now. We don't get cold weather now, do we? Now there used to be a canal that ran from Trent Vale to Newcastle-under-Lyme and that was a regular skating area from Trent Vale into Newcastle. I remember, I never did it, but I've known a chap that has done it many a time, a mile-and-a-half to two miles, easy. But it isn't happening now, the weather seems to be changing.'

Changing it may be, but Billy remembers some very cold weather in more recent times. 'It is about six or seven years since it has stopped us.' For several years it has been Ken's job to keep an eye on the canal and being conscientious he did not work to rule, but would be out on a Sunday afternoon checking the state of it. 'I used to walk along the canal on a Sunday morning, get a stick and walk along the canal and if it was getting thick I'd ring a boatman, "Come on, I'll meet you at two o'clock after dinner." We used to come for about three hours along the canal to try and keep it open, but a few years ago when it was eight to twelve inches thick, it stopped us for a month. It had gone to 28 degrees [Fahrenheit] in Shropshire, which is the next county, so you can imagine how thick it was.' Billy confirms, 'It takes about a week continuous, 'cos it's got to be really cold for about a week then it starts to freeze.'

Ken is sympathetic towards Billy and points out, 'Everybody forgets when they've seen him in the summer and he's brown and just got his trousers on, there, no shirt, "Oh, he's got a good job, we're here sweating, making the 'ware." I say to them, "Don't forget him in the winter, when you're in the nice warm factory, he goes along the canal,

The last load of chinaware was loaded in May 1995.

when it's raining, snowing or whatever." They never see him then, because nobody ever comes out!'

The catamaran was the last working boat on the Caldon Canal to carry chinaware and Billy and Ken are proud to have been associated with it during its last days. They each have one of the last plates to have been fired at the Potteries, with a commemorative note on the reverse to remind them of the 'last boat for china' and they joke about the leisure craft which they say are passing through more and more frequently. 'They have to take off their chimneys as they pass through the lowest bridgehole under Eastwood Road, and the girls sunbathing would scrape their tummies if they weren't careful!'

Their joking is an attempt to hide their sadness at the decline of the relationship between the canals and the Potteries. They remember the story of the man who long ago started Johnson Brothers: 'Like when Mr Johnson would go to church every morning at eleven o'clock and on Fridays he would cross the road to the factory and all the old pensioners would be standing in a line and he would give them all a sixpenny bit . . . Yes, times have changed in more ways than one.'

WOMEN OF THE BARGES

'It was the women of the barges . . . the queens of these little kingdoms, dark-eyed, gipsy-looking, weatherworn creatures, with shawls over their heads and children crawling about their feet, who stood at the doors of their cabins as they have stood for generations, patiently waiting for the next move onward in their wandering existence. The smoke of their domestic hearths went up from the little chimney before their faces, their babies crawled on the deck beside the chimney, tethered with string and next door to the inevitable lark in its cage; their elder children clambered among the cargo and all about the narrow vessel which was their home and nursery and school and playground; their only neighbours were the people of the barge which happened for the time being to be tied up beside them; the tiny cabin before them, a few feet square, and not high enough to stand in, held all their worldly goods, their kitchens, their romances, their bridal-beds, their husbands and babies, their past and present and all their future. . . .

Mrs Green, like most of the older boatwomen, was dressed in black – a long black dress down to her ankles, black stockings, and thick black boots like a man's. She wore at her throat a large photograph of Mr Green in a brooch, and from her ears dangled large ear-rings of green glass. Her hair was bound tightly across the top and round the back of her head in six or seven thin plaits. . . .

Just inside every door on the left-hand side were fixed a few shining brass knobs and bosses, like the ornaments of bedsteads and carthorses and, highly polished, they made a brave show. Some cabins had only two or three brass knobs, and some a dozen; at holidays, when times were good, the lady of the boat would buy another brass ornament or two, and

A young canal-boat lass from Brentford. (National Waterways Museum)

by the number of brass ornaments the knowing might know if the family were prospering steadily or not.

Old Mrs Green had seventeen brass knobs, and when the sun shone in through the door the cabin was dazzling. Beyond the brass knobs was the tiny stove, polished and speckless . . . and on each side of the stove were hung festoons of ornamental plates – fine decorated plates with gilded edges or filigree borders, and pretty pictures of Victorian ladies or dancing shepherdesses and in great gold lettering, 'A Present from Bombay' or 'Banbury Cross'. A glittering brass culinder was over the stove, and among the plates were hung little brass ornaments – a tiny

Women trainees on board the boat Ascot in 1944. Although met with some opposition, a training scheme was started during the Second World War enabling women to undertake war service by operating canal boats. Mainly middle-class women were enrolled and they often complained about the primitive living conditions. (National Waterways Museum)

brass anchor, a candlestick, a cannon, and a big brass spoon. Over the small hanging lamp was a burnished shield which shone like the sun. Beyond was a cupboard which had a castle on the door, and was fringed with framed photographs. . . . Opposite the stove was a low chest or locker which served as a seat; then came a curtain draped back during the day, and hung with more photographs, and behind it the bed. The bed let down out of the wall, and nothing was to be seen of it by day but a panel and a castle, and in the bed-space was kept a small trunk and a broken gramophone. Not one inch in this Lilliputian home was wasted for service, yet every inch was a decoration. To the stranger peeping in from the lock-side it seemed no more than a kennel, a doll's house, but if he sat inside for a few minutes it seemed to expand. . . .'

from 'Up the Cut', *The Water Gipsies*, P.A. Herbert, 1934.

Chapter Seven

THAMES WATERMAN AND BARGEMASTER TO HER MAJESTY THE QUEEN

ROBERT CROUCH

Robert Crouch wearing the livery of Bargemaster to Her Majesty the Queen

In the City of London, at the bottom of St Mary-at-Hill, is Watermen's Hall, headquarters of the Watermen and Lightermen's Company. It is an unobtrusive building, but at the stone entrance stands a waterman wearing the striking red livery of the Company. Inside, the entrance hall is sombre but the glass cases, protecting a vast array of silver trophies and artefacts associated with the River Thames and its famous watermen, lighten the atmosphere.

Just off the entrance hall is the office of Robert Crouch, Bargemaster to Her Majesty the Queen. From behind his large and imposing desk, Robert Crouch begins to tell of his life on the 'royal' waterways, his natural friendliness imbuing his tales with charm and nostalgia. 'One of the most vivid memories I have of my childhood was when I was about three. We were living at that time on the Isle of Dogs, my father having married the daughter of a stevedore over there. He was home on leave at this time and the house was hit by a bomb. I remember being rowed across the river to Greenwich where his mother lived. The dog, a Dalmation, was on a piece of string. I remember all the barges on the river being alight.' Bob became animated and his voice rose. 'It seemed the whole of London was on fire! I don't think I was really frightened, but it was something that would register in a child's memory.'

This is the earliest event Bob remembers on the River Thames. He was born on 14 May 1937, at Shooter's Hill, South London, a 'third generation waterman, which in watermen's terms is a relative newcomer. Most working watermen can trace their families back certainly to the Fire of London, but then all the records at Watermen's Hall were lost. My father took over from my grandfather, he was the first waterman in our family. He came from a Kentish family, but he was apprenticed to a Mr Ridley to learn the trade of waterman and he eventually became an attendance waterman at Greenwich Buoys. In those days, of course, it was rowing in skiffs. "Attendance" meant that when a ship arrived fully laden with cargo it was moored by the attendance waterman and then throughout its stay he would attend on it with his skiffs, taking the crew and stevedores and various people to do with handling the cargo from the shore to the ships, backwards and forwards.'

Bob's father took over from his grandfather, still using the skiffs and oared vessels, and at one time the family had four skiffs moored inside Greenwich Pier, but times were changing and it was his father who instigated the move from skiffs to motor boats. Nevertheless, Bob still remembers his early introduction to working with the skiffs on the river. 'I was about eleven when helping to row the stevedores off in these skiffs to the ships. . . . I did intend to take over from him, but containerization was taking all the cargo trade from the London docks down to Tilbury.'

Like many fathers before him it was not Bob's father's wish that his son should follow him on to the river as he felt there was not a great future there, so he encouraged him to stay on at school. Bob had shown a flair for technical drawing so his father set up an interview for him with a firm of bridge-builders. However, Bob was attracted by what he saw as the glamorous life of working on the river and during the lengthy period between leaving school and the interview, Mr Crouch senior decided he would give Bob a second string to his bow and apprenticed him at Watermen's Hall. 'The interview grew nearer, but was not mentioned until about a week before. "I can see you don't want to go for this interview, but my advice is that you should. All the same, if you really want to stay afloat and finish the apprenticeship, I will allow you to do so," said my father. I never went for the interview.'

The River Thames was the main highway of London in the sixteenth century and it is said that 40,000 men once earned their living rowing cargo and passengers on the river. The watermen of those days were the taxi drivers of today's London and operated in passenger wherries. Unfortunately, there were problems. So rich and successful was London as a port, that a sailing ship would arrive and, due to congestion, would have to queue for weeks before it could get onto a berth. When the crew were idle and off pay they would very often use the ship's jolly boat, row up into London, fight with the local watermen, set themselves up and take their business. They were frequently joined by boatmen from other English rivers and even from the continent. These interlopers used inadequate and unsuitable boats, were inexperienced and did not know the tides. Safety and order were at a low ebb so in 1514, when petitioned by the watermen and citizens of London, Henry VIII passed an Act of Parliament and set up rules to govern the river and the watermen. With no one to implement this legislation this was something of a failure, so in 1555 another Act of Parliament set up the Watermen's Company with nine rulers, honest men of substance who owned their own houses. 'We did not become part of the proper Guild system of London, the Livery system, although we join with them. Ours is quite a nice position. We are a bit like the ship's cat; everybody seems to like us, from top to bottom.

'The river was the natural arena for any big celebrations. On those occasions the livery companies and other companies would have very large barges, rowed by eighteen, maybe twenty men, on which they could celebrate and go afloat. There was the City barge which was the Lord Mayor's barge and the barges of the various livery companies would follow, particularly on the day the Lord Mayor was inaugurated. The numbers of the livery companies came from the position of their barge behind the Lord Mayor's barge. That's where the story of the Skinners and the Merchant Taylors, No. 6 and No. 7 comes in. Well, apparently they could never agree as to which was to be No. 6 and which was to be No. 7. They argued and argued and one year, in the procession, the two barges had a fight with each other. Very embarrassing for the Lord Mayor, so he called their masters and he said, "Now, in future you will alternate. This year you'll be No. 6 and you'll be No. 7 and next year you will change over," and that's how the phrase "all at sixes and sevens" came about.'

Through the Watermen's Company an apprenticeship scheme was set up and watermen had now to be licensed. A licensed waterman wore an armbadge with a number on it and if this was reported by a dissatisfied passenger, the badge could be forfeited.

'In those days, the apprenticeship was one year.' Bob looked thoughtful. 'Gradually, through the centuries it altered for various reasons. One year was not really suitable, particularly when the Victorians embanked the river and made it much narrower and the tide regime much harsher. To know the tide sets and all the things that affected the river needed longer.'

As trained sailors, for many years watermen were the target of press-gangs, but fortunately apprentices were exempt. The apprenticeship was gradually built up to seven years and not only did this ensure the men were properly trained, but it protected them from being taken into the Royal Navy. Eventually the Watermen's Company collaborated with the Navy, to provide men on a more organized basis. 'Our most famous press-man was, I suppose, Shillingford, Nelson's coxswain who, though pressed into the Navy, was used by Nelson for all the ship handling because that is the business of watermanship. In fact Shillingford was killed by the same cannonball that took off Nelson's arm, so to us, Shillingford is one of our famous watermen.

'Essentially, we are still doing the same thing that we were set up to do. We still have an apprenticeship system. We still bind a boy and master together at a binding ceremony when the indentures are torn in half and they both keep their own half, which will always match and prove that they were the two that were joined. Just think back, in early days there could be as many as five or six hundred apprentices a year. This year we had twelve, so there has been a great change, but basically we are doing the same thing.

'The master's job is to teach the boy, his apprentice, his work and after two years he comes before the court at Watermen's Hall and after the full five years he has an oral examination which lasts about forty-five minutes. He is asked all sorts of questions on watermanship and, of course, nowadays lightermanship which is a slightly different business. It is pretty terrifying. The apprentice comes with his master, and the master tells the court that he is satisfied with the boy and he is ready to be examined. He then sits back and the young lad, or girl nowadays (we have four women going through), they have to stand and answer the questions fired at them by all these old grey beards sitting there as a court. They are asked questions on everything; navigation, tidal regime, paperwork that's involved, safety. A whole range of things that will be necessary for them when operating between The Waterman's Stone, at Cliff in Gravesend and Teddington Lock. That's the licensed area. You never forget it. In my days there were about twenty examined on that particular day and we had to queue on the tightly winding staircase of this Georgian Hall and as you wait there the tension builds more as you get nearer the door. The lucky one goes in first and the unlucky ones later. Mine went very well. My father was my master and he was pleased and we went off afterwards to the local, as they all do, and had a few jars to celebrate.'

Bob was now a qualified waterman, one of the boys, doing the job he was cut out for. He was happy. He had enjoyed his apprenticeship and his father had got him into a firm called Silvertown Services. 'They were the transport division of Tate & Lyle, the sugar people. So the cargo was raw sugar, finished sugar, molasses, and the famous syrup that they used to make. I was unloading raw sugar from the ships into barges and bringing it to the refineries where the finished products were being made, then up into the docks and delivered back to the ships. Although we did, and still do, teach our apprentices to row barges, to drive barges as it is called, with oars or sweeps, it is all done by tug now. So the barges have to be worked off to the tug in deep water and then the tug will take them to wherever they are going and the lightermen will take them into the wharves or docks to be unloaded. Most of the docks would at some time or other have ships loading sugar for different parts of the world. The raw sugar mostly came in at Purfleet. So 300-ton barges went down to Purfleet; six of them behind a tug, towed up. They unloaded into the refinery the white sugar, or the molasses or the golden syrup, which was in cartons at that time.

'There were two refineries, one at Woolwich, which was called Tate's and another a little further up the river called Lyle's. We worked between both of them. There was also a residue, great mountains of demerara sugar in sacks that had been stockpiled at the side of the docks during the war. A lot of this stuff had hardened and it was in a terrible state and this was called "cut and shoot". This meant that the stevedores, or dockers, had to cut each bag and shoot the contents into a barge. This was very long, hazardous work. They were three-hundredweight sacks. Great sacks of sugar, which had been laying around for years and years and years and all that had to be cleaned up and cleared up and put through the refinery. It was still used, it was still usable. Oh, yes, even the sticky syrupy molasses that was at the bottom was taken up and put through the refinery. Nothing wasted, no.'

In his first year of freedom from his master, Bob took the opportunity to row in the oldest annual sporting event in the world, known as 'The Doggett's Coat and Badge Wager'.

'Doggett was an actor,' Bob explained. 'He was described as a comedian, a political comedian, making comments about Parliament and everything else, no doubt. He was a Whig and very pleased that the new Hanoverian King George I had come to the throne. In 1715, which was the anniversary of the King's first year of reign, Doggett wanted to do something to mark the occasion and he did what a lot of people did in those days, he inaugurated a race on the river. They gambled on anything in London in those days. They were great gamblers and one of the things they would gamble on was matching waterman against waterman, in their wherries. A prize would be given for the race, it might have been a silver armbadge,' Bob gestured towards the silver armbadges from the past decorating his office. 'There might also be a back board for the winner's boat painted up to say that the waterman had won a particular race. They might have been awarded a bright coat, a red coat, a blue coat or whatever, or even a whole boat, a wherry. In today's terms it was like a taxi driver winning a new taxi. Of course, from a waterman's point of view, to have a nice silver badge, or a nice bright coat, or back board, was a good thing because when he was plying at the stairs for passengers they would think, "Oh, he must be safe," because he had won various races. Anyway, Doggett decided to inaugurate his race and it is the only one that has survived, due to the good offices of the Fishmonger's Company who became Doggett's executors. They preserved his will and his race and it has been raced every year since 1715. So in my year, 1958, we had five entries. This was instead of the full six as there was an illness on the day.'

The watermen's families were very proud if they had a young man, a nephew or son, competing in the race, but in the preceding days the palaver could be overwhelming. Bob's mother used to say, 'I'm fed up with Doggett. I have him for breakfast, dinner and tea.' The race was taken very seriously. 'It's not one of the things you can take lightly, because you've got to complete the course, which is four miles, five furlongs. You've got to practise. We rowed. It was a sculling race, unlike the Norfolk wherries which had sails. The name wherry comes from the shape of the underpart, they are a shallow draught and they can float in very shallow water, as do the sailing wherries of the Norfolk Broads. The Watermen of London's wherries were very cleverly designed. They were banana shape, so they would ground and as the passengers walked back to take their seat and then sat down, their weight would lift the boat off and the waterman would have less pushing and straining to do to get afloat.

'For the race there is one man to each boat, no coxswain and no passengers. He rows with two oars and, in the very early days, against the tide.' Bob looked affectionately at the model of a wherry standing in the centre of the mantelpiece and went on to explain the rules of the race.

'Doggett set the rules of the race, supposedly on an incident that happened to him one night, when leaving the theatre on the Southwark side. There were no watermen plying for hire at the stairs there, so he came over to the stairs on the other side of London Bridge. They are still there today. They are now covered or blocked to some extent, but they are still there, next to London Bridge. Well, he could see six watermen with their lights on, with their torches ready for hire, but it was a strong ebb tide and the wind was down river as well, and when he asked to be rowed to the Swan Inn, Chelsea, where he lived, five of them refused and dowsed their lights, but one young lad, who was just free of his master and a new freeman, said he would do it. He rowed him that distance against the tide and all the elements. So, Doggett said in his rules of the race there will only be six, in memory of the six men that were available, but they will have to be young men, just free from their masters and they will row from London Bridge to the Swan Inn at Chelsea and that will be the race. The prize will be, he actually said an orange coat in his will, upon which will be a silver badge and he donated the value of the badge, and that was how the race was set up in the first place.'

Racing on the river was very popular and because of the rich rewards, there were those who would bend the rules a little to give them a better chance of winning. Through the Watermen's Company, Henry VIII had appointed Beadles, inspectors who would measure and inspect the licensed boats for 'tickling'. 'Yes, tickling was a means by which somebody who was a pretty good oarsman and fancied himself in the races, would try to lighten his boat by thinning it down by sanding or planing away the planks to make the whole thing as light as possible. It gave him a better chance of winning, but of course in doing so, he made it dangerous and even more dangerous for his passengers, so it wasn't a thing that was encouraged.'

Bob won Doggett's in 1958 and his winning time was twenty-eight minutes 'and a few seconds' he added modestly. 'It is always about half an hour.'

The same year, his apprenticeship complete, Bob went off to do National Service. It was not usual for National Servicemen to join the Royal Navy but Bob, irritated at the prospect of serving in the Army, persuaded the organizing committee that he was more suited to 'the water' and fortunately he was enlisted in the service of his choice. 'I think they rather confused watermen and lightermen with their true profession because they put me in the electrical mechanical division!' Bob joked heartily. 'But I was very lucky. I saw some sights, you know, I got about a bit,' he grinned, a twinkle in his eye.

Bob shakes hands with a past winner of 'Doggett's Coat and Badge Wager' in 1958. Bob's father is the second from left, wearing a hat (Sport & General (Press Agency) Ltd)

When Bob returned to work he joined his father for a while and then he had a chance to get into bridge piloting. 'I rather liked that. It was quite glamorous. My father said, quite rightly so, that it was a dreadful job, having to work all times of the day and night. This is because you are working with the tides, but I did bridge piloting and a bit of dock piloting for about seven years. A bridge pilot takes over from the Trinity House pilot who brings the ship up the middle of the river, then the bridge pilot would take over from him and pilots the ship through the Thames bridges. When you think there is up to 25 ft rise and fall of tide twice a day, you can see that this is something the captain of the ship wouldn't have any knowledge of, so the pilot, who has local knowledge, comes on board and takes him safely up through the bridges.'

Bob went on to become involved in civil engineering and construction work, but it was becoming clear that the newly built container docks and quays at Tilbury were draining the commercial activity away from the Thames. With this in mind, he took the decision to stay in London rather than go to live and work in Tilbury and his next move was to the leisure industry. 'I applied for a job as skipper with a pleasure boat operating from Westminster Pier and could see immediately that there were all sorts of opportunities here. It was on the threshold of being something quite big. . . . I bought into a newly formed company called Catamaran Cruises and that gave me a seat on the Board. Gradually I managed to buy a controlling interest and built the company up from one boat until, I think, it was the biggest company on the Thames. It had seven operational boats, a floating restaurant and three piers on the river.' Catamaran Cruises was slightly affected by the recession, but remained a prominent company and a surprise awaited it. 'Almost out of the blue, we had a French company approach us about buying us out. I, like the other four directors, was approaching my late fifties and we thought this was an opportunity not to be missed, so we decided to sell. Part of the deal was that I had to stay on for two years as chairman. It is now a very successful company and brings boats over from Paris. There is a Parisian way of doing things. We used to tailor-make parties for individual clients, including food, entertainment, everything, but I think there are more clear-cut options for what people can have now.'

Bob chose an appropriate time to apply to become a Royal Waterman. 'It is the thing to have won Doggett's and this rather gives you the edge on the river. You don't have to do these things, but if you have done this or perhaps have a successful company, have proved yourself in some way, then you can write to the Lord Chamberlain's Office offering your services to the Queen as a Royal Waterman. You get an answer, of course, saying that they thank you for your offer and they will put you on the list. And you wait. I waited eight years, but normally it can be fifteen years and some become too old while they are waiting and never get through. It's restricted nowadays to twenty-two Royal Watermen. It's a proper Royal Appointment, you know, you get the Lord Chamberlain's Certificate, signed today by Lord Airlie and from their number are chosen, by the Palace, the Royal Bargemaster.

'This all dates back to when the monarch, like all rich families and companies on the river, had his own river transport and, of course, the King's barge was very highly decorated. You can see some of them down at the Greenwich Museum. They've got a complete hall dedicated to Royal barges. The Royal Watermen would row and the Bargemaster would be Captain of the boat, as it were, but then he was a courtier. The Bargemaster's uniform today reflects that he is a member of the royal household. He wears a red tailed coat with plastron front and back, whereas the Watermen wear typical watermen's dress which is a frock coat, again in red, with plastrons.' Bob explained that the plastrons are worn on both the back and the front of the uniforms, rather like a

Royal Nore, *Her Majesty the Queen's barge. Robert Crouch, Bargemaster to Her Majesty the Queen and the Royal Watermen are on a royal river duty. (Port of London Authority)*

breastplate. The silver-gilt is embossed with an emblem of the Crown, and today, the insignia ERII.

As Bargemaster to Her Majesty the Queen, Bob usually carries out about seven duties a year, but this year, 1995, he has been exceptionally busy. Most of the duties are on the *Royal Nore*, which is maintained and operated by the Port of London Authority. 'I am notified by the Palace that the Queen will on such and such a date, be travelling from such and such a place to wherever, and I have to liaise about the *Royal Nore* and lay on, if it is the Queen, eight Watermen and Bargemaster. If it is, for instance, the Prince of Wales, he gets six Watermen and Bargemaster, but the Queen must agree because they are her Watermen and belong to the Queen. They are the Queen's Watermen and she is quite fussy about who she lets use them. Obviously this is all arranged for her through the Lord Chamberlain's Office, but she takes a keen interest in all the regalia and ceremony and she would spot if she had one Waterman short, or one too many. She is noted for being very observant on the ceremonial side.'

Bob's duties are very varied, but all are important. 'I had a Royal duty yesterday when, quite unusually, the Queen let the President of Finland, who was here on a State visit, use the *Royal Nore*, and because it was part of a State visit, he was allowed six Watermen and Bargemaster and we gave him a ceremonial tour of the river. The Victory in Japan celebration was one for the memory book. It was a fantastic event. The Queen travelled down from Lambeth and disembarked at the Royal Yacht which was laying in the Pool of London. Part of her progress was followed by little veteran ships from Dunkirk days and a whole procession of people in boats.'

Once the river was a vast arena for a wide range of events, from weddings and funerals to all kinds of regal celebrations, but much of this has moved away from the river and this is reflected in the duties now carried out by the Royal Bargemaster. 'Two of the duties that used to be carried out by barge and Royal Watermen on the river are now done by carriage, but the Watermen have followed ashore. Now they man the carriages on the State ride when the visiting grandee is received and driven with the Queen in carriage procession to Buckingham Palace. The Queen has her own men on her carriage, but we man some of the other carriages and I have to lay on up to ten Watermen for that.

'The most important thing we do as Royal Watermen is the State Opening of Parliament. Originally the crown jewels were kept at Hampton Court and one of the duties of the Bargemaster, for many centuries, was to take the crown, and the crown jewels, for the State Opening of Parliament, by river, in the Royal Barge to the Houses of Parliament. Of course, that changed over the years.'

One of the main reasons why many of these activities and events, like the Lord Mayor's Show, were driven ashore was 'because the river was used as a sewer,' said Bob in defence. 'It was called The Great Stink, and people just couldn't bear to be near it. So a lot of these duties migrated ashore. Now, taking the crown to Parliament is still done by the Crown Procession, which goes off ahead of the Queen's Procession, taking the crown and maces, and cap of maintenance and the sword of State to Parliament from Buckingham Palace. We take it ahead of the Queen, and I actually get to hold the crown for about thirty seconds every year and, as everybody asks, yes, it is quite heavy. It is quite a privilege when you think that only about five people get to touch it. When we get to the Victoria Entrance of the Houses of Parliament, the jeweller unclips it from its place in the carriage and gives it to me and I take it across and hand it to the Comptroller who takes it into Parliament to be made ready for the Queen when she arrives.'

Robert Crouch will retire as Bargemaster to Her Majesty the Queen in May 1997, but it is quite obvious that his love of the river still remains. His memories recorded here depict a period of great change and excitement, and the upholding of a great tradition which will, hopefully, never die.

THE FIGUREHEAD CARVER

Jack Whitehead sitting by his recently completed figurehead of the Earl St Vincent.

In the yard in front of Jack Whitehead's workshop on the banks of Wootton Creek, stands a huge colourful figurehead; an 11-ft high effigy of Admiral Earl Saint Vincent. 'He ran away to sea at the age of thirteen and then became first Lord of the Admiralty. Worked his way up.' Figureheads were once the hallmark of many a great ship and until the 1960s they could be regularly seen on working ships, sailing the lower reaches of the Thames. In 1985, Jack's partner, Norman Gaches, carved the last figurehead and nameboard for a commercial Thames riverboat, a catamaran called *Naticia*. Today many figureheads are carved by Jack and Norman to adorn historic reconstructions and Jack has become familiar with the history surrounding all his carvings.

Jack was born on 18 March 1913 and has seen both the demise of ships bearing figureheads and the revival of these magnificent artefacts. He has always had an interest in ships and been fascinated by figureheads ever since he was a child, but he never thought that one day he would be able to carve such objects.

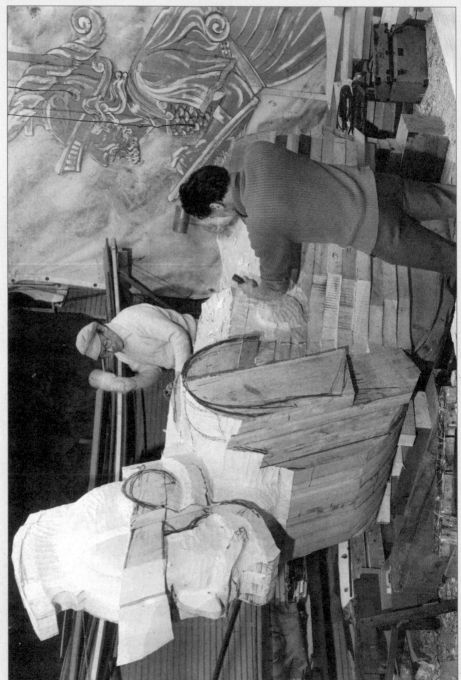

Carving a new figurehead for HMS Warrior.

Jack at work on the figurehead for Falls of Clyde.

'I got injured during the war and couldn't use my fingers, but to get them moving again I started to do woodcarving . . . toys, then furniture and puppets.' Many years later Jack decided he wanted to learn something about boats and he and his family moved to the Isle of Wight. 'I got a job in Uffa Fox's old yard in Cowes. I did carving and made masts and rudders and all sorts of things.' He went on to carve a figurehead of a mermaid, for a friend who had built a yacht, and then Jack and Norman did demonstrations of figurehead carving at the London Boat Show for several years. Jack had not realized there was such a demand for figureheads and no one was fulfilling it. Commissions flowed in. 'We got wonderful jobs like the big figurehead for the *Warrior*, the first iron-clad battleship that we had in this country. It is laying at Portsmouth now. It's an enormous ship with a white figurehead on the front that is 15 ft high. The next job was wonderful too. A big sailing ship that had been built and launched in Scotland in 1877 and was being restored in Honolulu. Sir William Lithgow approached me and said they wanted a figurehead and they wanted it carved in England by an English carver. "Would you like the job?" "Would I like the job?!" I replied. So I carved it right here and it took about five months altogether. I was carving for a very big ship, nearly 400 ft long.'

Jack had to go to Honolulu to finish the carving and to adjust the figurehead to fit the ship. He then went up to Scotland, to Lithgow's shipyard where the ship was built, to do some research. Wherever possible, Jack likes to research thoroughly the project he is working on. While in Scotland, he became involved in making a film about the ship. 'I made an appeal asking for anyone who had souvenirs or anything connected with *Falls of Clyde*. That was the ship's name. It was one of nine ships all named after waterfalls in Scotland and this was the last one left. It was extraordinary. An interesting souvenir was from the Isle of Islay. A man had had passed down to him, by one of his ancestors who had been a carpenter on board the ship, one of the earliest photographs of the ship. The photograph showed that right around the stern was a big stern carving.' This was the only record of this available and from the photograph Jack was able to carve a 56 ft long thistle design that stretched right around the stern.

Another of Jack's commissions was for the sail-training ships of the Sail Training Association that come in and out of London taking young people on sail-training voyages. 'They needed figureheads, so we carved them and I remember we had a lion on the *Winston Churchill*.

'They've got a big collection of figureheads on the *Cutty Sark*. They found the figurehead from the *Cutty Sark* in pieces down in the hold and they saved it and asked us to go up there and have a look to see if we could rebuild it. When we were asked if we would like to restore a few more figureheads, I asked, "Yes, but what do you mean by a few?" "Well, rather a lot really; thirty-seven altogether." So over the years, Norman and I have restored thirty-seven of the *Cutty Sark* figurehead collection. They are still there now.

'If a figurehead exists, it is usually in a terrible state and we have to rebuild it, but if you're starting from scratch it's a bit complicated, because the owners of the ships might want to see drawings. What we usually do, we often make a rough model of the bow of the particular ship from drawings and we model the figurehead in plasticine because a lot of people cannot visualize it in three dimensions if they only see a drawing. When it's approved, it's a matter then of taking careful measurements of the bow of the ship where it has to fit and then you literally have to glue up a great block of yellow pine with epoxy resin glue, before you start to cut it. We get the timber imported from

The completed Earl St Vincent.

A figurehead of a woman. This was the first solo venture by Jack's grandson, Daniel Whitehead.

Canada. There's one firm in the country that imports it and it's beautiful timber to carve. Most of the old figureheads were carved in pine. Well, it's a matter of taking away all the wood you don't want and being very careful about it.

'We try to get the original colours on an existing figurehead. They usually have coats and coats of paint on and sometimes you can scrape it down. Well, we don't know what they were like when they were painted because most of the photos of figureheads were in black and white, but we do try to find the original colours. The figureheads like *Falls of Clyde* and those great wind-jammers were usually painted white with a little colour and a little gilding. Sometimes it can be just a question of using one's imagination. When the whole thing is more or less carved, it gets a soaking in wood preservative which the old figureheads didn't get. Then it is a matter of painting. We might put a white undercoat and sometimes two or three top coats of good yacht paint and it seems to last. Gilding is done with gold leaf. There are two types of gilding. One is transfer gilding where the gold leaf is on a thin tissue paper. For this you have to use gold leaf size which has to be just right, not too sticky and not too dry. Just right. Then you take this off the thin tissue paper and there's your gold. It is not a difficult thing to learn. Then there is another gold leaf which has to be burnished with an agate too, but it is expensive stuff.'

Even though his hands are gnarled and sometimes quite painful after a lifetime of hard work, Jack is still carving and says he has no reason to retire. When he considers how it was a wartime injury that set him on his path he says, 'It's an ill wind that blows no man any good.'

Chapter Eight

TUG CAPTAINS AND TOM PUDDINGS

LEONARD WALLER AND BRIAN GREGSON

Brian Gregson

It was a bitterly cold day in January, a Saturday, and the canals of the Aire and Calder were deserted apart from an occasional moored boat. Len Waller and Brian Gregson paid no heed to the cold. Since they were youngsters they have been used to being out in all weathers. Len, the elder of the two men, the son of a bargeman, is seventy years old and has now retired from his life on the northern waterways, but he still feels part of the scene and is keen to tell of his life on the water. 'I was about sixteen when I went on the boats. I went on barges, but not with father, although we were both on barges.'

Len became accustomed to barge life at a very early age. As he was one of eight sons, his mother was pleased to send the younger of her lads off with their father in the school holidays. Len smiled and chuckled knowingly, 'We couldn't get into much mischief with him because he was always watching, but father would take us on the barge and we would play football down in the hold.' The old man's thoughts turned to clothes, an important consideration in such a large family of boys and they were expected to take care of them. 'When we were lads we used to wear corduroys. They were hardwearing. Later on, working on the barges, we wore sealskin, which wasn't very expensive in them days. Yeah, and moleskin, on t' boat, waterproof you see. We wore boots,' he continued thoughtfully, 'but them old boatmen, they used to wear clogs and they didn't wear socks inside. There was no reason for going without, it was just their way.'

Len remembers starting work as if it were yesterday. He wasn't nervous and by the time he was sixteen years old he was no stranger to life aboard. 'I went as a mate with Blundy Clarke's, at York. There was two of us on a boat and you used to get towed about with a tug. We used to carry anything, coal, beans, tobacco, anything. Then I had to go into the Army and when I came out I went with Wilby's carrying coal from different pits all over West Yorkshire. The wagons used to come up and tip the coal down a shoot and it used to go on the boats. Later it would be unloaded with a crane that grabbed it, but before that, there was a big bucket and we used to have to shovel it in.

'I worked with "Tom Puddings", but only for a bit. They are a thing of the past now.' 'Tom Puddings' were container vessels designed in 1862 by William Bartholomew. Tugs would go backwards and forwards between the collieries and Goole, shunting and shifting these vessels. 'Today there is a lift, a barge tippler, the biggest in Europe. It has an enormous capacity and it can carry five 90 ton pans an hour. Up they go to a height of 30 ft and then they are emptied of their load of coal. It's a marvellous sight.

'Sometimes cargoes of produce would be unloaded from the ships and taken on the barges to Wakefield and Leeds and the other big towns. We took tobacco sometimes and that would go to the warehouse in Leeds. We could only get two big rolls on the barge and a barge would carry

100 tons, so they were very big rolls. Like great rolls of cable, they were. I can smell the strong smell of tobacco even now. The boats are bigger and more powerful today, but in those days the barges were of wood, 85 ft long and a '/ ft draft.'

At Knottingley, some men would be employed loading pitch. This was a miserable job and better carried out at night beyond the heat of the sun's rays. The fumes could be overwhelming and pieces of pitch would stick to the men's skin, causing irritation. It was a great relief when they were eventually provided with masks and protective canvas clothing.

Len remembers the days when the barges were horse-drawn. 'We had horses at Wakefield. There used to be one horse to a barge and there would be a chap that would look after the horse. He stabled it, the lot, and he would walk along with the horse, but the horses knew the way. They even knew the changeover bridges. They are not so fussy about keeping boats smart now, but the horses were very smart with their brass polished up and they were well stabled and looked over at night. The locks shut up at night so we couldn't go through the night.'

It is the lock-keepers who ensure there is enough water in a canal and this can sometimes be up to 8 or 9 ft deep. 'Quite deep,' says Len. 'The canal doesn't alter much, only a few inches. With the river it is a different matter. If they have rain up in the Pennines the river can swell and rise by as much as 5 ft in a very short time.' Like most adventurous young men, Len occasionally took chances as a lad. 'When we used to run from Nottingham in flood time and if we were in a hurry to get back, we would go straight over a dam instead of going through locks.'

In Len's day the lock-keepers were not paid and they depended on the tolls they were allowed to collect. The bargemen would give them a penny for letting them through the lock. 'They were known as lock pennies and we would get them refunded by the barge owners when we got back. I remember one time when my pal Maurice, just for a lark, heated up the lock penny until it was red hot. He threw it on the lock side and when the keeper picked it up he had a few words to say I don't mind telling you.'

Len tells of how 'some of these big ships of Harkers had problems with head draft if they were unladen. They built them too high, so they used to fill them with water to weigh them down, so they would go through t' bridges at Goole and then they would pump it out once they were through.'

It was an accepted part of the job that bargemen would be kept away from home. 'We were away from home three or four days at a time, maybe, and we would sleep on board. We might travel through the night sometimes, but it would depend on tides. Tidal current stops at Naburn and right at top of Trent.'

Later, Len was on tankers for a while and then he finished his working days with Cawood-Hargreaves. His mate was Brian Gregson who eventually became a tug captain in his own right.

Brian was born in Thorne, near Doncaster. He is a large jolly man, fond of life and he enjoys being on the northern waterways. When he started work he did three months down a pit, but he soon tired of that. 'In those days you could leave your job and walk into another one right away, but you don't change willingly in this day and age. After pit I went on barges, in general haulage. It was a Sheffield size craft. The length was around 65 ft. Boats were built for the area they covered. They also built boats to go to Lincoln which were a bit longer, but they were a bit shallower. Nottingham boats were a bit longer too, and they were also a bit shallower.

Brian Gregson aged sixteen and just starting work.

'There was once a number of independent operators and a range of vessels. Now there are not too many firms. Cawood-Hargreaves, their barges move in teams of three and carry about 500 tons when fully loaded. Where once there was a total of sixty-four staff, including maintenance and office staff, there are twenty-eight now, yet we move more coal now than we did then. There is a petroleum company just started running from Hull to Leeds, and one or two private barges running sand and gravel to Leeds.

'Yes, you can still get yourself a boat and start work. You have to have a licence for the boat, but not for the crew. The hardest part is getting the work and to find it. There is one chap who bought up a couple of

Loading tanks for lime. This was to be transported only a very short distance away to the sewerage works, but water was the only possible route. Brian is second left.

barges to do up himself. He did one up and he was earning a living carting sand and gravel. I think he is doing the other one up now, but it must be difficult having to undercut the price and all. There is so much to do with all the life-saving equipment and that, that you have to have these days.

'For the first few years I was running around, I never came up to this area, it was more Rotherham and Sheffield. Generally we were taking corn, but we had loads of iron ore, fruit and peanuts. By the way, there was an unwritten law that said you could always take a little bit. KP peanuts were a favourite with my dad. The odd bag of sweepings that I took home did wonders for the hens' diet and he could boast the biggest and best birds come Christmastide.

'The lock-keepers too, used to have a bit of coal and we gave them a bit of corn which perhaps we had wiped up. Most lock-keepers at that time were not on a big wage so they used to do a bit of gardening, growing vegetables and keeping chickens and we used to get bits and bats off them in return.' It was all part of the privileges and a great way to build up camaraderie between these men of the northern waterways who have always been known to lend a hand and help each other out of any difficulties. However, they also played pranks on each other too.

By the time Brian became a tug captain it had become the tradition to toss a penny to the lock-keeper, although it was no longer expected 'When we used to come through Pollington Lock the lock-keeper's

Pollington Lock where the little dog picked up lock pennies to save the lock-keeper coming out. (Fallings Lock Boatyard)

little dog used to pick up the pennies and take them to the lobby and give them to the lock-keeper to save him coming out to pick them up. One day I happened to say to him, "Good dog that." "Yes," came back the reply, "but he don't pick up silver." "What do you mean?" I said. "Well, he don't pick up sixpences or shillings. Try him." So I threw 6*d* down. The dog picked it up and took it to him, so all he'd done were to rip me off, like.'

Over the years the men's working hours have become more regulated, but at one time Brian worked very long hours and he, like Len, spent a lot of time away from home. 'In 1963, when I was a lad, we used to set off early in the morning if we had to deliver the load the next day. I've set off at five o'clock in the morning and it's been six o'clock the following morning when I've got to Sheffield. We'd work right through. Got a cup of tea, had an hour's kip, a man would knock us up, we'd get unloaded; twenty-five hours in all and we'd set off back. We got £3 10*s* a week wage and ten bob a trip. Sometimes I used to go away on a Sunday or Monday morning with a little bag of grub and depending what time we'd sail, it were lucky if me mam see me the next Saturday.'

'I was on the *Alpha* at the time, for Bill Gillyon, and what he used to do, he didn't pay me a lot of money, but he kept me well. I'd take me little bag of grub and he would buy some fresh meat or eggs, or something, during the week. If he went out to the pictures he would take us too.'

As time went on Brian got to know the various tricks of the trade. 'What we used to do when I was with a bigger shipping company, we used to get loaded at Hull and set off and at that time of day you used to get to Goole. All kinds of craft, including coasters, and there must have been fifty waiting to put into Goole at that time, and you would be talking to the lads, "Who are you for? Where are you going to?" and if it were the same place as yourself you would ask, "Well, what time are you going?" They would say a time and we'd reply, "Yeah, we're going about the same time," but next morning, you would get up about an hour earlier. You would let your ropes go, so not to make a noise with starting up the engine and you would pull the boat by hand until you got clear of all these other boats and set off so they didn't hear you and you could beat them to unloading point. Then you could get unloaded and get another load before they did.'

It could be quite a lonely life on the boats for an extrovert and sociable character like Brian, so he was sometimes glad of the opportunity to meet up with the lads. 'It didn't always happen that way, sometimes you'd say where you were making for that night, "Well, we're making for Goole, we'll see you in the boozer." We all used to gather in the boozer and tell tales of one thing or another. They were good times. Other times down at Hull, you may be waiting to load, so you'd get a bus into town and go to the pictures and afterwards come back to the boozer for an hour. When Lennie and me were together they were just daytime jobs. I never actually worked with Lennie when we used to have nights out, but yes, they were the good times. Them days there was plenty of work about.'

Unlike in Len's day, with this new affluence there were more opportunities to get home at night. In the 1960s the Morris Mini made its first appearance on the road. Perhaps it was his status symbol, or perhaps he was really eager to get home at night, but Brian joked about one chap who used to take his Mini on his barge. 'He was skipper of a barge and he used to take his little Mini on the barge, put it on the aft deck so that he had always got it with him when he wanted to go home. I should think he was the first chap in this area to take his car with him on barge. If he tied up halfway between destinations and he wanted to go home, he would just drive the car off. He'd got ramps to do it with.

One skipper took his Mini on his boat with him. (Fallings Lock Boatyard)

Just drive home, drive it back next day, put it on and off he'd go again. He were a bit posher than everybody else. Other people would have little motor bikes, even push-bikes.'

Over the years, safety has become a more important consideration on the waterways. Len's brother seriously injured his neck and broke his collar-bone when on board a sloop at Goole and, 'he still had to cycle all the way home'. Brian says that safety precautions have been tightened up, but he thinks that rules for the provision of life-saving equipment on privately owned boats are less stringent, 'in fact, sometimes non-existent'. The big shipping companies are more attentive, Brian says, but he remembers an incident in Hull docks when he brought about his own little disaster. 'We was doing a bit of painting. We used to have a piece of life-saving equipment called a "Carlafloat". It was made out of cork and it was for clinging to, not for sitting in. It was an oval thing and the centre was open with slats across. Well, we used to put a hatchboard across them and use them for standing on while we were painting the boat. Well, you will do anything like that when you are sixteen. Well, of course, it turned over and I went underneath and I had to be pulled out by our skipper because, would you believe it, I can't swim! And I've never learned my lesson and I had a couple more escapades when the same guy rescued me. The tanker people have to go through lots of courses for health and safety, radar and steerage. That's clamping down. That's when you're working the Humber. 'It's a hell of a lot easier to work 'em down there now,' Len reminded him. 'We never had radar, we just had a compass to work with and that were it. Foggy weather and all.' But Len is one of the old school, fog or no fog he seldom resorted to the compass for assistance and never had a serious accident.

Len still thinks of the waterways as a working area and is sometimes anxious about the safety of the new leisure-time sailors who have not learned the rules. 'The lamps on a boat are for people to see you, not for you to see the way, but these leisure narrow boats with big spotlights on, all they are doing is causing hazard to the other people because they are blinding them.'

'On the whole there have been few major problems,' says Brian, but accidents do happen occasionally, in spite of the precautions taken. 'We once had a breach at Caroline when it flooded the mine at St Aiden's. It was open-cast coal, top side of Castleford. National Coal Board at the time. Our firm Harkers, used to distribute it, so we used to go there to load. Now I think the Coal Board got too greedy and got too near the river bank and consequently the river wasn't wide enough. Breached and flooded the mine. Now, they always blamed the river for breaching its banks, but people have their own opinion on that. They should have known. It started flooding on Saturday morning and for three days the river was running backwards. All traffic stopped. It was a marvellous sight to see the river running backwards from Castleford Lock. At Castleford Lock, where it takes it into canal, the river goes across. It is a crossroads. If you go straight across you go to Wakefield, if you go right, you go to Leeds and if you go left, you go to the old weir and back into the river behind you, and all that water was running upwards to the open-cast mine.'

There has been a decline in the amount of freight transported by water in this area, but Brian feels that this need never have happened. 'It was all due to them in Hull forever calling dockers' strikes. Now Goole Docks, Immingham Docks and Grimsby Docks, they never went on strike, but Hull did and they was thriving. It was as soon as they started having strikes that they started deteriorating. The BACATS [A Barge Aboard A Catamaran], they were built for the river, but dockers didn't want that, they thought it was doing them out of work. They would have been floating containers that floated straight into the ship and were taken away and never came into dock, but because the dockers were causing so much uproar, they agreed to run them as conventional craft and bring them into Hull, loading and unloading them like a conventional barge instead of doing what they were built for and floating them into a sunken ship. The ship would come into the entrance of King George Dock and fill up with water. Ballast down with water. They would open the doors at the front and float the containers out, or BACATS out, a big tug would take them. He'd put in what he had brought down, a changeover, and away he'd go. I think he only come twice and then carried on in a conventional way.'

Brian is obviously sad at the outcome of what he feels could have been the saving of commercial freight in the north. Nevertheless, he believes in the future and looks forward to the days when he hopes the northern waterways will, once again, be vital arteries for commercial freight.

HARRY STEVENS AND THE WEY

Only a few navigations remained independent of railway companies and government control, but some continued to stay in business. The Wey Navigation, which is known to have been improved by Sir Richard Weston in 1651, was one of these companies. Its most recent owner, Harry Stevens, perhaps through luck or sheer determination, managed to stay independent until he bequeathed his charmingly canalized river to the National Trust in 1963.

The Wey Navigation has been connected with the Stevens family of Guildford since 1812, when William Stevens became lock-keeper at Trigg. His family became the owners of the Navigation and Harry Stevens continued to manage it right up until the 1960s. He disliked motorized craft and still used horse-drawn barges, specially built for the business by the Edwards family at Dapdune. The banks of the waterway were protected with timber only where absolutely necessary, and he retained a number of the turf-sided locks of an earlier era.

The family all took an interest in this tranquil waterway. No doubt it was quite rural when Dapdune Lea was built in 1894 for Mary Jane Stevens, the sister of William Stevens III, and a cottage for their neighbours, the Edwards family, the barge-builders, was built just along the lane.

Harry Stevens can be said to be responsible for preserving the rural qualities of the waterway for posterity, although the growth in the number of pleasure boats has caused the National Trust to replace some of the older parts of the canal.

Chapter Nine

THIRTY YEARS
ON THE
WEY NAVIGATION

VINCENZO LOCATELLI

Vincenzo Locatelli

It is thirty years since Vincenzo Locatelli came to Send in Surrey to work on the Wey Navigation; he had no particular ambition to make his living working on the water, even though his father was a sailor. However, he was drawn to the canals and their mysteries at an early age. 'From childhood the canal was my playground and environment. I grew up in Camden Town, North London, and the Regent's Canal and Hampstead Road Locks were where we played, so I suppose my interest in canals has grown from that. Ever since I was a child I was aware of the narrow boats and the horse-drawn barges and the barges generally on the Regent's Canal.'

Vince built up a business and owned several commercial narrow boats on the Regent's and Grand Union Canals; however, few things in life are permanent and eventually he decided to make a change. 'We had two young children while on the narrow boat and that was home for the first two until we moved down here and then we had two more. At the time we enjoyed living aboard and it was quite an acceptable way of life, but it would be a pragmatic fabrication to say I was just dying to work on the waterway. It was due to circumstances.'

It was becoming increasingly difficult to find work for the boats, but for Vince and his wife, their family was their first consideration and Vince emphasizes: 'We came here purely and simply so that we could moor the craft and my eldest child could go to school. My ex-wife and myself had discussed whether we would carry on on the canals and educate him ourselves. She was an educated woman and perfectly capable of doing so, but we decided that would be a selfish attitude.'

Built in 1651 by the local landowner, Richard Weston, the Wey Navigation is among the earliest of the historic waterways. This nineteen mile stretch of waterway still retains much of its rural charm and has changed little over the past two centuries. Lush, open water-meadows flank its banks, and here and there are woodland groups of graceful pollarded willows and clusters of alder. Old turf-sided locks, weirs and lock-keepers' pretty cottages are dotted along the tranquil banks of this most southerly of the inland waterways, yet this is not to say that it has not known busier times. Once Wey barges carried Surrey grain along this stretch of water into London and returned laden with coal from the Thames wharves.

Perhaps it was destiny that drew Vince to the Wey. 'In the fore of the boat that we lived on, I had carried an odd-shaped windlass and the only thing I knew about it was that it operated a lock south of the Thames.' Vince and his family now live in the National Trust cottage which overlooks Worsfold Gates Lock. This has paddle-gear, once common on the Wey, but now perhaps unique. A particular handspike and windlass were used by the crews to open these gates and it was these implements that Vince had carried on his narrow boat for so long.

A friend told Vince of the vacancy on the Wey and he was very enthusiastic about it. 'We were given *carte blanche* mooring. Pick what you want and do what you want, so long as you work on the waterway. If somebody had said to me then, that I would be still here in thirty years' time, I don't think I would have agreed, but that was that. The National Trust had only recently taken over the waterway and that was in October 1965.

'I was an assistant to the Navigation Foreman, very rapidly became his charge-hand and within twelve months had taken on the job of Navigation Foreman, which is the position I have held since. It is difficult to define the duties. I was standing on the bridge at Catteshall up there and there was a group of schoolchildren and one of them asked, "What's your job? What do you have to do in your job?" I looked

Discussing the next move at Stoke Lock in 1980 are, left to right, David Way,
Vince Locatelli and Ern Eggar.

and I thought, "Well, if you can imagine standing here and if you drew a circle, everything that comes within that circle is part of my job. The bed of the navigation, the canal, the banks to the tow-path, to the fences, to the trees, over the top and down to all the locks, weirs and bridges. Boats too, are all involved. Keeping them all in working order and to liaise the whole lot together so that the waterway functions effectively.'"

The protection and maintenance of the banks is one of Vince's many tasks, and although some things never change, it is a natural waterway that he is dealing with and unforeseen things do crop up, so it is a question of adapting and dealing with them as they happen. 'When I first came here there was a lot of vole activity. This has always been the bane of the canal-maintenance person's life in so much as voles work very near the surface. Even a minor fluctuation of water level causes water to run through and the vole holes can very rapidly turn into breaches. Well, years ago there was a constant alert for vole activity, but that's been eased over the past fifteen years by the increase of mink along the canal bank and while voles and mink are learning to live with each other, the voles are getting through to survive, despite the mink. Nevertheless, it has cut down the vole activity and released maintenance staff from what was once quite an onerous burden.

'The method of dealing with the vole trouble, when we got it, was to excavate the vole tunnels and to reconsolidate the bank. Over the years various methods have been tried to stop the activity; crushed glass, or a solid seam, that is a timber plank through the middle of the tow-path, but one way or another they always got the upper hand. They operate just above the waterline and then they go down into their burrows and it is that which causes the problem. We spent lots of time trying different methods to compete with them, but we never succeeded and then along came the mink and solved the problem for us. Of course, while mink are regarded by many as a menace and an

Vince taking measurements on Walsham Weir.

intrusion, the habits of mink and the fact that they cover a mile stretch, means they are self-limiting. Mink, rather like kingfishers, cover an area, their territory, and that limits numbers.'

Vince paused. He seemed pleased that nature had found a way of solving its own problems, rather than man finding it necessary to intervene and exterminate the voles. He went on, 'I don't think I can say that mink are a menace. In many respects they have become part, while they are an alien part, they have become part of our environment and I see it as a valuable part, because they have solved problems for us.'

Areas of high activity, such as the approaches to locks, Vince explained, must have 'hard protection', the interlocking of sheet piling, for example, but other areas are soft landscaped. 'For many years we had a local expression for soft landscaping, which we called "Barnarding". This involves removing a luxuriant growth of weeds from one area and taking them down to other areas to encourage new growth so that you get self-perpetuating bank protection. The reason why we called it "Barnarding" was because when Dr Christian Barnard performed the first heart transplant, we were working with a boat alongside us and on the roof of that boat was a small radio which was entertaining us while we were carrying out what could be described as an arduous task. They were reporting that Dr Barnard had for the first time successfully transferred a heart from one person to another and we were in the throes of transferring weed. From that time onward, the task became known as "Barnarding".

'It's a very successful way of protecting the bank. What we do is, at a certain time of the year, which is usually during the growing season of May, June and July, we take the weed *en masse* down to other areas and peg it into place and encourage it to grow there. Once it starts to take root, we usually put some dredging silt or other material over the top to stabilize it and it takes root and goes on growing. Quite considerable lengths of the Wey have been treated in that manner over the thirty years that I have been doing it, but I also hasten to say it is not a new idea, it's not something I originated, it's an age-old method. It's a method of bank protection which has been in practice for many, many years. The old canals were dug on a trapezoidal section, shelved, and weed was planted along the margins because of its beneficial effect.'

In 1812, William Stevens became lock-keeper at Trigg's on the Wey Navigation and his barge-owning family acquired the waterway in about 1900. Eventually Harry Stevens endowed the river to the National Trust. A year later, Vince took over the care of the Stevens's sixteen miles of waterway and, in 1968, the Commissioners of Godalming Navigation handed over the remainder.

When Vince came to Send in 1965, he felt the Navigation had been well cared for, although some unessential maintenance had been a little neglected. A lick of paint here, some grass to mow there was all that was needed and it seemed to have been loved and cared for. Vince laughs when he looks back to what he thought when he first arrived. '"Give me a couple of years, five years at the outside, and I'll have all this up together." I think it was the flush of youth. Thirty years later and I am still grappling with the problems, but I think it is fair to say that the National Trust has taken great strides forward in those thirty years.'

It was once rumoured that Harry Stevens was an eccentric, a birdwatcher, who would not cut down trees. Vince has a great deal of sympathy with this man's priorities but, nevertheless, he knew that certain treework had to be carried out for the benefit of the waterway and the trees themselves.

'There were a tremendous number of overhanging trees. I remember when I first came up here on my narrow boat, the chimneys and everything were continuously knocked off the cabin roof by the overhanging trees and branches, but I think that it would be untrue to say that it was a derelict waterway. The predominant waterside trees are alders and willows which are, in effect, waterside weeds. They are larger than the normal concept of weeds, but they are in fact waterside weeds and they require constant husbandry. The willows, which are specifically planted, are kept pollarded and the others, which are natural generation, are cut back and tidied as necessary. The alders, which generally self-seed, are kept in check and what would appear to be severe pruning is beneficial with alders, particularly in so much as it encourages healthy young grass and the attractive appearance of the waterway.'

Vince also looks after the beds of the Navigation and this is done by dredging, which has sometimes brought up some intriguing finds. 'Occasionally we de-water and we will physically go along and remove obstructions. Things such as tyres and debris, but I have pulled out six or seven safes. They have always been drilled and emptied. Obviously the result of some criminal activity. They are surprisingly heavy to move. The first one I came across was many years ago. In those days the police diving team used quite regularly to come to the Navigation for practice dives, so I notified them that there was quite a large obstruction which would probably make a good practice exercise and they came out and they actually recovered it. It was obvious when it was recovered that it was a safe and it had a large section of the back removed. It was quite a sizeable one, so it was not surprising that we couldn't physically move it without a recovery vehicle.'

Maintenance of the boats as well as the waterway itself is another part of Vince's job. There are thirteen, sometimes fourteen, Trust craft. Some of them, such as the dredgers, are for specific jobs and others are more general-purpose craft used in the overall maintenance of the Navigation. These are described by Vince as 'the wheelbarrows of the waterways'.

During his time on the Navigation, Vince has become extremely fond of the Wey and likes nothing more than to delve back into the history of the waterway and its craft. He was naturally delighted when asked to take part in the recovery of the wreck of the Wey barge, *Reliance*. He now laments, 'At the time it was merely a job, but in retrospect a very important job, and I am sorry I did not do more to record the event. When they first told me they had located an old Wey barge down at Leigh-on-Sea, I said, "Oh, yes, I know Leigh-on-Sea like the back of my hand, I went down there a lot as a youngster," but when I went down there again, I was suddenly confronted with the new sea wall and that Marina place that they've constructed there, and it was only when I was by the station that I knew where I was! Anyhow, when I found it, I instantly recognized it as a Wey barge. I knew it from when it was

The Reliance *awaiting salvage from the mud-flat on Leigh-on-Sea, Essex.*

working and it was involved in an accident in 1968 on the River Thames and then taken to Leigh-on-Sea for scrapping, but it was purchased by somebody at Leigh and used as a store for many years.

'It was in a derelict state and it was donated by its owner to the National Trust and then, on behalf of the National Trust, I organized its recovery from Leigh-on-Sea, its salvage, refloating and towing up the Thames back to Dapdune Wharf, Guildford. We patched it up and refloated it and towed it up the Thames and it was in quite a sorry state. Yes, it is one of the original old Wey barges, 80 ft long overall with the rudder, by 13 ft 10 ins. A big one and very fragile as it had been involved in an accident twenty-five years previously. It is being restored now, down at Dapdune Wharf and is a prime exhibit.

Reliance *was built at Dapdune in 1931–2. She is 74 ft long and once carried 84 tons. Her last cargo of wheat was from London docks in 1969. She has now been restored and can be visited at Dapdune Wharf, Guildford.*

'The barges used to work the Royal Group of Docks, the George V Docks. The final barge traffic on the Wey was from Cox's Lock Mill, which is just above Weybridge, down to the Royal Group of Docks. They were only back traffic. They weren't taking anything down river. They used to just bring grain back up – American Hard and Canadian Grain – and they finished in 1968. There was a slight commercial revival in 1972, but that wasn't with barges.'

Dapdune Wharf was once an important barge-building yard when the Wey barges were built, so Vince took great pride in bringing the barge back to that particular centre. 'I also supervised the reconstruction and restoration of the wharf at Dapdune. One of the things that is particularly gratifying is that I'd kept the old capstans and the old equipment from the dock away over the years, and we were able to re-use those and set the dock up and pull *Reliance* out in the old method, as they would have done the old barges years ago. It made an interesting project, using the ropes and blocks, sliding ways and capstans.' Vince hesitated as he pulled himself away from this historic avenue and explained, 'Sliding ways, that is where the barge was actually hauled up on timbers, sideways, on to the dock, and we were able to set that up again.' He looks modestly upon the part he played in supervising and coordinating the procedure and emphasizes, 'there was a terrific input from other people and it was very much a team effort'.

Vince has been involved with a great deal of reconstruction work along the Navigation and his plans follow a somewhat unconventional procedure. 'I have plans and I have the same habit today, and it's thirty years on. I have pieces of folded paper in my shirt pocket, with all the details on them. I used to work out the details and the key details, the strategic measurements, were written on these pieces of paper and kept in my top pocket. The rest of it was in my head and I always had the ability to see a completed job in my mind's eye.

'That reminds me, when I was on my way up to rebuild the Riff Raff Weir, we had borrowed from Mr Stevens, or, as we called him "the old man", one of the old wooden barges and it was an ex-Basingstoke barge called *The Fleet* and it was my idea to put a big frame and a derrick, to be able to drive the piles across the river to de-water the area and to rebuild the weir. Well, we were on the way up the river on the old barge and I was steering the barge and I had a young chap by the name of "Ginger", Peter Duffel, who was tug skipper and to give credit where credit is due, he was quite a good tug skipper. Now, on entering the canal at what was then Plummers, and is now Debenhams, in Guildford, it is sharp to port, or to the left, and then into the canal entrance, but Ginger pulled the tug rather severely into the canal and caused the barge to race towards the high wall of Debenhams. I saw the barge racing towards the wall and it came into my mind, "It's not our barge. It's the old man's." I ran forward to try to fend it off because these are old wooden barges. My efforts at fending it off were unsuccessful and the barge hit, with a resounding *Sssssmack!* and the ricochet, as the barge moved out, left me standing in mid-air, and I went straight down into the water and came up underneath the barge. I thought, "I'll kill him when I get my hands on him." I was immediately aware that all my details and measurements for the reconstruction of the weir were in my top pocket. Well, I had Wellington boots, thick socks, donkey jacket, heavy jersey, because it was midwinter. Well, when I finally came out from underneath the barge which was lying at an angle across the waterway, I looked up and in the sudden light there was the sheer wall, the steel piling and concrete of the side of Plummers and the side of the barge. I swam to the starboard end of the barge and I was able to scramble, like a drowned rat, over the rudder and up over the cabin top and down into the barge. By this time Ginger had reappeared and his first words were, he always called me Squire, "What's up Squire? The barge's gone aground." Of course, without me on the tiller the barge had gone aground on the end of the island at Millmead and it was then he realized that I was somewhat wet and what had happened. My measurements too, had to be deciphered!'

Nevertheless, Vince thoroughly enjoys his work and he even finds time to laugh at some of the strange things people do when they are learning to navigate their new leisure craft along the waterway. 'Nothing, nor nobody on the Navigation is a nuisance. The very essence of our being is to provide a waterway that people can enjoy at all times. There can be the odd time when there can be a degree of embarrassment because of the actions of one or the other. That's ourselves included, but no people are a nuisance.

A day-boat on the Chelmer and Blackwater Canal. The design of barges varied from waterway to waterway.

'I have been fortunate that for thirty years of my life I have done a job which I have thoroughly enjoyed doing. I have never found it a hardship to get up in the morning to go to work. That is the reason why, instead of working a thirty-eight hour week or whatever, I now end up working a sixty hour week: it's a way of life, not a job. It changes, it's varied and sometimes you can get fed up. We have had a period just recently when we've been working in mud because of the floods and so on and when the end of the day comes you look back, and you feel the sense of achievement from the day, well, that's that.'

Chapter Ten

THE CORACLE-MAKER OF THE SEVERN

EUSTACE ROGERS

Eustace Rogers by his workshop

The village of Ironbridge takes its name from the iron bridge built in 1791 that spans the River Severn a few miles north-west of Coalport. In the shadow of the bridge on Severn Bank lives Eustace Rogers, coracle-builder. Everybody around knows Eustace. Just Eustace Rogers, Ironbridge, on a letter, will find him. His house is more or less on the same site as the house where his father's family lived for generations, but it was rebuilt by Eustace and his father, a little higher up the bank.

Eustace is very proud of his family who have been working on the river and constructing coracles there since long before the iron bridge was built and he enthusiastically recounted his yarns about them.

'I was born the day the First World War started, 5 August 1914. As a matter of fact some of them old ones used to blame me for the First World War,' he joked. 'I was born up the street. Me mother's family lived just up the street and that's where I was born. Somebody came down the street and they said, "He's born" and somebody else said, "Start the war then."

'Now me grandad was the biggest poacher in the world. Big in physique as well. He was eighteen stone and he feared nothing in the world, he didn't that man. He took the last barge down 106 or 107 years ago. It was a load of fire-brick from a brick yard. You see the area was so rich in minerals. That is why it all began here. You see they'd got everything; ironstone, coal, clay, limestone, it didn't matter what, it was here and so was the means of getting it away. In the very early days, when the only power was water and wind, the brook up here, the Dale Brook, was driving the bellows and the forge hammers for the ironworks, you know. The whole area was Coalbrookdale, right down to Coalport was Coalbrookdale and the canal on the top there, a couple of miles away from here. Now out there is known as the Coalfields; Coalbrookdale, Lightmoor, Dawley, Ketley, all that area, because the coal is so shallow, with no depth of soil on it, it was known as the Coalfields. Now the coal was coming along the canal, if you have heard of the incline plane, with the full one going down, bringing the empty one up, well, this was the incline plane, bringing coal from the canal down to the barges on the river. That's how the name is derived see, Coalport, because the coal was being loaded there, and it was the busiest inland port in the whole of the country, Coalport was. One writer said he counted sixty eight vessels waiting to be loaded with coal down there. I'd say there were four hundred on the river in all.

'It's easy to say I wish they'd done this and I wish they had done the other with regard records, but we must remember, there was very few that could put pen to paper. Now me grandfather couldn't. He couldn't put pen to paper, so what chance had the earlier ones than him got, but I can remember me grandad making the coracles here. I was ten when he died in 1924 and he was eighty-one, but me dad, he would talk about his grandfather making them. See the family's been here before that bridge. That's in the family bible, earlier than the bridge, and I'm sure it goes earlier than what is recorded, only as I say . . . nothing was recorded at that time, but afterwards you wish you had recorded it.

'I used to go to the school on the bank known as the Blue School. I was doing something every night after school. We were always getting driftwood. They said we were foragers. Me dad got his living in the countryside, rabbit-catching all his life and we were getting the driftwood off the river and that's how we went on, working every minute, but enjoying it. Wouldn't have changed it for anything. Yes, me father was a rabbit-catcher and I started going with him from the age of eleven and I couldn't leave school quick enough to go with him. Well, I went with me father. I left school in the July. I wasn't fourteen 'til the August. Well, he didn't start rabbit-catching 'til perhaps about the third week in August and then he'd finish at the end of March to let them breed again. You see the farmer didn't want that farm to be infested with rabbits, but you did, being a rabbit-catcher.'

Eustace spent the winter working with his father, but then the estate was sold and Eustace told how the timber fellers moved into all the woods and felled too many trees all at the same time. The rabbit population decreased and there were not enough to give father and son a living, so when Farmer Thomas asked Eustace to help load the hay in the violet field, on his father's advice he stayed with him for a couple of summers until he became cowman for another local farmer.

'Now there was seventy cattle. Thirty-five milkers and thirty-five young ones. . . . I looked after them cattle for twelve year. Never had a day off. Every weekend, every Christmas day, every Good Friday, just the same for twelve year. I never thought I'd leave him. He never thought I would, but we had words and I went to the next farm and I was with him for many, many years. Then I went on the River Board, keeping the banks clear of falling trees that looked like tumbling into the river.' Wages were low and Eustace was glad that he was able to earn a bit extra doing the jobs he knew well. 'Whatever job I was doing I could still catch rabbits and I did coracles all those years, but there was not the demand for them in those days.'

Unfortunately, myxomatosis stopped rabbit-catching for a while, but when Eustace retired from his last job at the power station, he was glad to be able to 'have more time to concentrate on what I enjoy doing'.

Eustace took pleasure in making coracles, just as his family had done for generations before. A coracle is an oval lightweight wicker boat, covered with waterproof material, which is used on lakes and rivers. 'You see the coracle is the earliest known boat. That's how they describe it. They don't know anything earlier. It was a working boat and none more so than with the net fishermen. You see it is the ideal thing for net fishing. See you can manhandle it with one hand and you got the other hand free to ply your nets and it's a little boat that you can carry up the river, see. I've been with me dad and me uncle and carried it from here to Hatcham, ten mile, and they'd be fishing coming down, bringing their wet nets and the coracle and the fish, bringing it to home. Now if they'd started here and went down, they'd got all that to carry back again, so they fished above where they lived.

'In my earlier days it was a working boat. It seemed strange describing such a slight craft as a working boat, but it was serving a purpose to help you to live. This was the thing, we were just living in those days, not millionaires, and this is where we have all gone wrong. If you saw a man with a coracle, it was no use of muggin' him! He hadn't got a bloomin' ha'penny, he was that poor. It wasn't only a working boat it was the poor man's boat. Now in this area, Coalport and Jackfield, it was much used to cross the river to save paying the toll to go over the bridge. The toll was only ha'penny to go there and back, but to get that ha'penny . . . oh dear. So that were much used for crossing the river for that reason. I've never seen them ferry. I've seen three in a coracle, but they have got to be two who know how to get in and out, or they are having you out as well, see. It's a very tricky job, I'll tell you. There were several here with them. Me dad said Jackfield people would be up and get a coracle for just a few shilling and there was a man just down there that used to make them too.'

Before a coracle could be made the materials had to be got together and Eustace explained: 'For years they were getting the material for them very cheaply and the coracles were only 10s each, p'raps. Then they got to £10 0s 0d.' This was partly because it became more difficult to get supplies of material and changes had to be made.

'In me dad's days, well up to the last few years of his days, we had used a local timber firm, Griffith's of Coalport, the next village. We call them splints, the strips coracles are made with. You wouldn't even keep any in reserve because it was so easy to get them straight away. Me dad would say, "I'll go down to Griffith's and get a set of splints", about twenty-four p'raps, to allow one or two to break and it was as simple as that. Well, when Griffith's folded up there was a bigger firm out here at Wellington, Groom's, an old-established firm, and he would go out there for them and then it really got difficult. They finished and we were even getting 'em from Welshpool. That far away. It became difficult and then afterwards, when I started on my own, there was a local man, a timber feller, and one day, he said, "We are felling some lovely ash, do you want some?" I said, "I do Alf, bring me some; 250 strips." That was some in reserve like, which as I said, me father never bothered, it was so easy to get it and finally, something happened. He worked for Groom's and when Groom's finished, oh, I'd go out to Creighton Arms and goodness knows where, Wem and Newport, and well, in the finish, I'd always ask for 250 strips. Well, they are only three-sixteenths thick. They were 8 ft long and 1¼ inches wide. Now that's a lot of sawing. A hell of a lot of sawing, and when they come to think they've lost as

Eustace with a coracle built by the Rogers' family method.

much in the sawing because the saw's quite thick. Well, in the finish the answer they gave me was "We no longer deal in small quantities." 250 was a small quantity for them, of course. So they would supply me with planks and I had to get a saw and saw them myself by hand and that's how I went on until two or three years ago.

'Wherever coracles were made, they'd got a different design. On the same river they'd be designed different. I don't know the purpose, whether each one thought their way was the best, or whether it was the only way they'd been taught to make it. We start off with the hoop first and we interlace the splints. The main method is, you fasten all this interlacing to the hoop. You've got standards for your hoop to stand on all the way round, at the height you want to make it. Then you bring these splints up to the hoop and fasten it all the way round. Shrewsbury didn't interlace their splints, but they made it on a mould. They'd got a mould the shape of the coracle and they made it upside down on that mould. And then, after they took it off, they would nail the splints where they crossed, they would nail them, but with our method we didn't need any nails.'

Eustace and his family preferred to use calico to cover the frame. 'There is a bit of give in it and it enables you to put something square on something oval, not many creases, see? See, canvas is heavy and there isn't this bit of give in it. No, I never see canvas used. We used ordinary wire nails. I can remember making one for somebody in France and he insisted that I should use copper nails. He said that any part that was iron would go rusty quick. Now for the tarring, now we have two gas works here and the tarring was so easy we would treat it with tar on the outside and the tar would impregnate the cloth. It was real easy to do. We would put a coat of neat tar on to impregnate the cloth and the next coat we'd put a bit of pitch and the next coat a bit more pitch to put a film on it, but you can't get gas tar now. We have to use bitumen and it's not so nice to use.

Coracle fishermen, Cenarth. (National Coracle Centre, Cenarth)

'It was one thing we never hurried. Me father used to say, if it was standing for a fortnight, that's better than it standing for a week. That's when it is in the skeleton form, you know. We would be working on two or three at the same time, doing a bit on this and then forget it and start another one. You see it's such a fragile affair we wanted it to set and take shape. Me dad always said, don't be in any hurry. Most of the work was done out here in the open, and stuff was stored in the shed. When you had got them in stages like that, there was always something on one of them that you could do inside if the weather was bad.

'Years ago it was cow skin. The skin is on the outside, with the fur inside, then it's fastened on with horse-hair rope, consisting of perhaps six horse's tails. We are talking about the very primitive man who perhaps hadn't got the means of cutting anything except with a very sharp stone or something like that. See, he wouldn't use the splints as I referred to, he would be using round sticks out of the wood and it had gotta be local to him because he couldn't go miles and fetch it. Well, that way of making coracles had died out, but I was asked, I believe the man wrote from Nottingham, "Can you make a Spey coracle?" and I said "Yes." I knew what a Spey coracle was, I'd never seen one, but I knew what it was and I wrote back and said, "Yes," and he wrote back and thanked me and said I would be hearing from a Mr David Hayes in Scotland. Sure enough, he wrote and said they couldn't get one made anywhere. I don't know to what extent they'd tried.

'Now it was going to Inverness. It was a visitor centre being opened there. A huge museum, but something for everybody's taste. He said, "It must be cow skin and horse hair." Now to be quite honest I hadn't bargained for this and I thought, "Well, now's me chance, a real challenge" and I wrote back, "providing I can get the materials, I'll make you a Spey coracle." I had a job to get the horse hair to be quite honest, at the time, but I got the hide from the local butcher, a mile away. I got the hair from the knacker's yard. I made it and it caused so much

Eustace with a Spey coracle.

interest locally, I thought I'm going to make another. I've made them now and they've gone to several parts of the world.'

This was a new beginning for Eustace; he had retired from the power station, the rabbit population was at a low ebb and coracles were no longer used on the river, but there was now a new interest in old crafts and Eustace was one of the very few men left to meet the demands of this small, but specialized, market. His coracles have gone to Australia, Mexico, Norway, Poland, Belgium, France and fourteen to Trader Vick's restaurants in San Francisco.

'We are talking about primitive man. He hadn't got a sheet, or anything, so they got the skin of an animal, but as time went on and they got the means of cutting the wood like I said, and having cloth to cover it, they would forget the hide and the hair because it's much heavier the old coracle is, than the recent one. As I've said before, the main feature to it is you could carry it miles, which they were doing regular, up from here to Hatcham, ten mile, you know and you were carrying that on your back. Now this old type, I expect that was about fifteen pound heavier. It's a lot, and not so handy on the water as the modern one.'

Today, because the coracle is considered so reliable, it is used frequently when a versatile portable boat is needed on a lake or river. It has proved useful for botanical surveys, water-sampling, animal rescue and by the National Trust for overseeing waterside archaeological sites. However, Eustace has some reservations about the people who make and demonstrate the craft and loan them out.

'Now a coracle-maker years ago wasn't showing anyone how he made it. Now if they want to make one, let 'em make one, but I can understand me dad and me uncle, well, they had to earn their living. I've thought a lot about this. As I say, there were many a tragedy on the river, and tragedies must have been going on elsewhere in those days, but this wasn't from coracles. Now if coracles had got into the wrong hands there would have been many more accidents, because until you've been with coracles that's the only way you know how unsafe it is. Me father, he was rigid on this, if you approached him, "Can you make me a coracle?" He'd say, "Can you swim?" and if you said, "Yes," "All right, I'll make you one." If you said, "No," he wouldn't absolutely refuse you, he'd say, "Now go and learn to swim and then come back again." Now I'm sure that deep down they knew that if they'd showed others how to go on, there would be many more coracles and I'd hate to think that I was linked with someone losing their life. I don't know how I would feel. In their day, the life-jacket was a big and clumsy affair, but now they'd hardly know they'd got it on, so I'm not so fixed as me dad. I don't ask if they can swim, but I tell them, I say, "now always wear a life-jacket and if someone else persuades you to let them get in, see as they've got a jacket." I think I canna do no more than that.

'A man come down here and got what bit of information he could, but before they knew what they were making, they were showing others how to make 'em. Having demonstrations, showing others. "Now," I said to one, "there will be a tragedy." "No, we always wear life-jackets." So I said, "Now there can be somebody from London watching you making them [on television]. How do you know what he's wearing? When he's made one, how do you know?" But they don't seem to care. They haven't witnessed the tragedy and the worst part of it is when you retrieve that body.'

The Severn is a very dangerous and unpredictable river and Eustace and his father, and grandfather before him, have retrieved many bodies. 'No one will ever see it like this again and they cannot visualize what it was like, but in the summer months, that river would be full of people swimming and trying to swim. This is a very dangerous river. Now what makes it so dangerous, you can be in up to your knees and the next step, you are perhaps in 12 ft of water. Now this is causing undercurrents, the water coming through such an uneven channel, this is causing

A ride with an experienced boatman. (John Simpson-Lee Collection)

undercurrents. Now I've seen some good swimmers drown in there. Now years ago when someone was drowned, that was a job for the police to try to get them out, but they hadn't got the facilities. The police would always come here and say, see what you can do. Now it's in the paper, when me grandad died in 1924, he had saved eight lives and he had retrieved thirty bodies. Now me uncle,' Eustace gestured towards a photograph of his uncle and his father hanging on his sitting-room wall, 'he would keep records and he said to me one day, "Now me and thee fayther, we have sat down and we have counted the lives what the old man had got out and what we've got out and it's around the eighty mark." Well, it's about ten that I've got out myself, so it's got to be ninety.

'The first one I got out were during the war, it was a little girl. Only about four or five. Bathing with the others and they never missed her. There were so many bathing together they never missed this little girl, but when they had all been accounted for, her clothes were on the bank. You know, a nice little parcel of clothes, and the inspector come here and he said, "There is a little girl drowned in the sand hole, will you see what you can do?" That little girl, when I took her to the side her father was there. Word had got to him and he'd come down. He couldn't stand up, the man couldn't when I took this little girl to the side. See, this is something they [the new coracle-makers] have never seen.'

Eustace was anxious to show his workshop in the shed on the bank below his house. He led the way down the garden path towards his display of topiary ornamenting the bank — a teapot, a dog and a duck. At the garden gate he stopped and again emphasized how treacherous the Severn can be and pointed to the mark at the foot of his garden wall. A small plaque marked the waterline of the 1946 flood. 'The biggest flood in living memory was 10 February 1946, but the records are here from 1672 and there's three higher than that and the major one was ten inches higher than the one that I say is the highest in living memory.

There was a lot of low-lying property then and funnily enough the people that were born in these houses and it didn't matter how often the water come in, they wouldn't go. They'd clean the house out and they wouldn't go and they'd see a house go [sold] that was high and dry, but no, they would live and die there. I've never known anyone swept away, but the big floods, the very big floods, what they was doing was washing the bridges away. This was the first time the river was spanned with one span, when they built the iron bridge, prior to that the bridges had been timber and stonework and perhaps they consisted of four or five arches. Now in those days you would see fully grown trees coming down the river during flood time and fouling these arches. It became like a dam and it was washing the bridges away.'

Such is the vandalism of nature, but Eustace has less patience with the vandalism of modern youth. 'Years ago they just turned the coracle upside down on the ground with the paddle underneath and they could be away hours and that would be there, but they couldn't do that today. It damn well wouldn't be there. It wouldn't be there five minutes.'

By this time we had come to the shed that was his workshop and Eustace told how that had been vandalized, 'It was a respected place that shed. We'd never got any money, but we'd got other things the locals would need. Somebody wanting a wheelbarrow, "Oh go down to Rogers'", somebody wanting a pick, a nailbar, anything, "Go down to Rogers'". The difference is, it was no use of wishing for anything in them days. I never heard me father, "wish this, wish that, wish the other". It was impossible. It was impossible wealth-wise, it was impossible to get more money than was possible. If you were working you got your wage which wasn't much, but for the last fifteen-odd years, it's been possible to start off with nothing and be millionaires soon. In no time. We've had the best of this world, I can assure you. I've often said it's better to be poor and safe, than rich and not safe. Yes, we've had the best of this world.'

THE NORFOLK EEL-CATCHERS

'I will tell you a little about the eel-catchers and their houseboats. The latter may be seen on most of the rivers hereabouts. The hull is simply an old ship's boat, standing high out of the water, with the sides raised, and a roof put over them, so as to form a house, or cabin, in which the eel-catchers live and sleep. The boats are usually painted white (or, rather, whitewashed), so as to be easily distinguishable at night, in order to avoid collisions, and also to be the same colour as the snow covered ground in winter, for wildfowl shooting. Eel catching is carried on in the autumn when the eels are returning along the rivers to again enter the sea; for, strange to say, the young ones are born in salt water, and then make for the rivers in the spring. The eel-nets, as seen hanging on the stakes, by the side of the huts, seem exceedingly complicated

Eel-spearing.

affairs, but are not so in reality. The whole net is somewhat like a traw net, has a mouth as wide as the river it is to be placed in, and tapers away to a small tail, to which is attached a movable piece, or "cod". The mouth of the net is fastened, at the two sides, by stakes driven into the river bank, which keep it distended; while a heavy chain is lashed to the bottom, to keep it in position on the mud. The top rope of the mouth hangs loosely between the two posts, so as to enable wherries or boats to pass over it. The top and bottom of the mouth of the net are kept from too wide distension by a couple of cords, which, by being shortened, will draw the mouth down as close as may be desired; so much in fact, as to close it, if necessary. Hoops are placed at intervals along the inside of the net, and to these are fastened transverse nets, having a small, pressed-up aperture in the centre, to allow the eels to pass through, but placed at such an angle as prevents their returning. The net finishes off with the above mentioned cod, a detachable bag, which, at intervals of an hour, is hauled up, taken off, and the eels contained in it emptied into a wicker basket or trunk. The mesh diminishes from mouth to tail, so that at the end a darning needle would stand a poor chance of getting through. Dark, wet nights in September are the times when the largest takes are obtained, and tons of eels are sent to the large markets in different parts of England during this month. Eels are also taken by spears or darts, mounted on long handles. They are easily managed; but care must be taken that the boat does not drift away, and leave you hanging on the handle of the eel-pick, with no alternative but a ducking. Choose a dark night for this sport.'

from *The Land of the Broads*, Ernest R. Suffling, 1893

Chapter Eleven

OLD UNCLE BILLY, THE WHERRYMAN

NIGEL ROYALL

Nigel Royall

A narrow, willow-lined lane gently meanders past holiday bungalows, along the banks of Hoveton Broad, to the premises of Royall & Son, Boat-builders. This business is owned by the family of Nigel Royall who, as wherrymen and boat-builders for the past two centuries, have known a tougher side of life on the Broads. As a child Nigel made himself useful by cleaning the boats and helping generally around the boatsheds and when he left school he trained at Alton Broad before joining the family yard full-time as a boat-builder. A splendid craftsman, he is the kind of man who would have excelled at anything he chose to turn his hand to, but there was never any doubt that boat-building would be his particular skill. He is a large, jolly chap, proud of his family and their connection with the waterlands. He relates with great pride both amusing and sad tales of their lives and the lives of their friends.

Nigel is particularly proud of his grandfather who started the boat-building business and his Uncle Billy; 'He was my great-great-uncle, my great-grandfather's uncle. My family have always been in boats, building them and hiring them. Years ago they were carrying trade cargos about and it was only when that finished and was all done with that my grandfather had to find another job and he went and got apprenticed at Jack Powell's in Wroxham. That were a boatyard and they built wooden boats. He didn't quite finish his apprenticeship, but he were certainly a good craftsman. He built a lot of good craft and he designed boats as well. Hire cruisers, you know, to do with the yachting side of it.

'My grandfather, and his father, and his father before him, going right back, had all lived in King Street. All the little yards were up there. Old barge yards. They were all watermen up there because that was a real old waterman's quarter. Anyone that were anything to do with the river in Norwich lived down King Street, and yes, my grandfather's father were on a wherry when he was three weeks old. His old man had taken him aboard and everything. He'd got his first skippering job at the age of eighteen from a man at Horning here, on a wherry called *Crow*, and he took his honeymoon on the River Chet in a little iron wherry.' It was not the custom for women to go on the wherries and Nigel's great-grandmother would only stay on board 'when the boat was light' [unladen]. As soon as the decks got wet she went ashore.

'In those days they were trading up the north rivers here 'tween Horning and Yarmouth and back . . . the rivers were split in two. You'd got the north rivers and the south rivers. Yarmouth is the middle bit. They didn't often overlap and if they did, if a Norwich river wherry come up here or one of ours went round there, there would be hell up. There would be a fighting and scuffling. Especially later on when trade was slack, because they felt they were poaching their trade. There was many a fight and set to over that.'

Nevertheless, there was great camaraderie between the men of the various regions and perhaps it was the old tradition of using nicknames that continued to keep this bond of friendship alive. The Danish Sea

Kings and their followers who settled in this part of the country, centuries ago, used cognomens like 'Sea Wolf' or 'Foam Borne', a custom that has been handed down through the generations. Nigel's friends and ancestors have included 'Blücher', 'Rats Bircham', 'Tubby Bunn', 'Hop-a-long', and so on, but woe betide the man who calls another by a nickname of which he is unaware. When one young lad innocently addressed a senior as 'No-neck', a name with which the short-necked man was unfamiliar, the terrified youth was chased by the irate gentleman for half a mile.

Cargoes became more scarce as the years went by and although the boats carried almost anything, the variety of goods diminished with the coming of the railways, the building of new roads and the improvement of road haulage vehicles. Nigel pointed out that his ancestors sailed in keels which were quite similar to a wherry. 'They had a square 'sal like a Viking ship in the middle of them and especially in those days they carried anything, people even, because that was the quickest way for people to get between Norwich and Yarmouth, on them. They'd either catch a lift or there would be a keel that would specially do that, you know. They were mostly doing malt, barley and corn for flour. Reeds, a lot of reeds because where they were cutting the reeds was often inaccessible for road traffic. Ice was a favourite cargo. There was an ice factory in Lowestoft and Uncle Billy would often pick up a load from the ice factory down at the harbour in Lowestoft. It's the Co-op now, but that used to be the ice factory. He used to go and get it and he'd go up King Street and sell it to the butchers and people like that. A lot of it used to go into the morgue to keep the old bodies fresh, so that was keeping meat both ways; a bit of beef and a bit of old human, like. Marl was brought from where they found marl pitch that they spread on the fields as a sort of fertilizer. Dutch butter would come from Holland and they would unload it from a big ship and they would load it on to the wherries and distribute it around the area. They might take back textiles from Norwich as a return cargo. Coal, an awful lot of coal was carried. That was one of the few things they could compete with the railways for, the poor old wherries. The coal used to come down from the mines in Yorkshire by railway trucks. There was a quay at Vauxhall in Yarmouth where they used to run these trucks along the quay and have these big old metal shoots down, and they used to shovel the coal into the shoots and it would run down the shoots into the wherries, and again they would take it off for distribution. Apart from that they came to have a hard time of it. Eventually, once they'd built the sugar beet factory at Cantley, there was a lot of sugar beet, because they were growing it on the fields and come the wintertime they'd uproot it all and take it round there to be made into sugar. Another trade they used to do a lot of, was broken stone for road-building, although the roads killed the wherries in the end, so they were doing themselves in really, but they used to cart that to a lot of places.'

Uncle Billy was the most notorious member of Nigel's family, and he had the reputation of being a tough old wherryman. He taught Nigel's grandfather to sail and his great-grandfather was also apprenticed to him. 'He was a bit of a rum old boy really. He would be on the go all the while. They would have to make sure they went with the tide all the while. If the tide was right for them at three o'clock in the morning, off they'd jolly well go. I don't know whether he was a bit fed up with it, but my great-grandfather got a job of his own and went off up to Horning and me Uncle Billy went off up to the Midlands somewhere, and God knows what he was doing up there, but he got married. He come back, but he left her up there. Then he got hitched up with a lady, Aunt Polly they called her, and she was a Bullen and she was vaguely related to the Boleyn's at Blickling Hall . . . Aunt Polly was quite well-to-do. God knows what she saw in him, because, I mean, he never

William Royall, or Uncle Billy, with Prince on Spray, *1933.*

washed nor anything like that. They had quite a big house in King Street, but they couldn't get married you see, 'cos he'd already been married up in the Midlands, so they just lived together. They had three sons, but one was drowned off his shed in King Street. The others went with Uncle Billy for a bit on the wherries because they used to sail with a man and a boy, but that was too hard work for them, not that the wherrying was too hard, although hard work it was, but because he in particular was a hard old man, my Uncle Billy was, so they left him and they took other jobs on the river elsewhere.

'In 1901, the year when Queen Victoria died, my Uncle Billy bought a wherry out Yarmouth harbour. She'd been sunk and he bought her for salvage. She'd come a cropper somewhere, probably a coaster or something had run into her and sunk her. That used to happen sometimes. He brought her all the way round from Yarmouth to Coltishall to Allen's Wherry Yard and he had them do it up for him. She was probably the biggest wherry they had out there, was me Uncle Billy's. Yes.

'I don't know whether he found he couldn't live on what he was earning on the wherry, but he used to do was were termed "truckin' and tradin'". You see, if you were carrying coal, the owners of the coal would say, "We don't mind you having a little bit for your fire in your cabin, but for God's sake don't go and sell loads of it off." But of course they did. It were obvious really, they were going to. A few sacks here and a few sacks there. They didn't earn a lot and his "truckin' and tradin'" used to get him up to all sorts of things really.

'My Uncle Billy was coming back from Haddiscoe and he was coming along and it was getting a bit late and probably the tide was turning and he thought he'd lay up for the night. Now there was this old boy had a field there and he kept ducks. They used to then, keep poultry and that. And he said, "Can I moor up here for the night?" Well, this old boy must have heard of my Uncle Billy, because he had a reputation, and he said, "No you can't, I don't want you anywhere near my ducks." They argued a bit and then Uncle Billy said, "All right then, I shan't." And so this old boy watched him and my Uncle Billy sailed away and this 'ole boy then went home into his cottage and my Uncle Billy lowered his sail, so he couldn't be seen above the reeds, turned the wherry about and came back. He come alongside and went in the field. There were 200 ducks in there and he broke every one of them's necks. Threw them on the ice, to keep them nice and cool, whipped down to Norwich as quick as he could, got 'em on a train up to London and he reckoned they were cooked and eaten before anyone knew they were missin'. 'Course the chap couldn't do nothin' about it. He knew who'd done it, but he couldn't prove anythin'. They got up to all sorts of tricks like that.'

Winter was a very hard time for the wherrymen, but Uncle Billy was a hardy man and took the cold weather in his stride. 'They used to put sacking round themselves, 'specially round their feet, to try and keep a bit warm. My Uncle Billy, he used to come back sometimes and would be frozen solid. He used to wear a sort of fisherman's smock-thing sometimes in the wintertime and they reckoned that was frozen and he couldn't move his arms. He used to come in and my Aunt Polly used to boil some water up and he used to stand in a tin bath of water, you know, and the steam would slowly thaw him out. But that was about the only time he ever did get in the bath. They'd sometimes hear a tinkling sound as they sailed along and that would be the river slowly freezing over. Yes, he used to get frozen in. Yes, me Uncle Billy on the *Spray*, they got frozen in. The ice got so thick they couldn't break it and he once got frozen in down near Cantley somewhere and he lay there for weeks. He had to. First of all, he wasn't too bad, he managed to survive on what he had with him, then he was digging mangolds up out the ground and eating them raw when he ran out of coal. I suppose he wouldn't want to leave the wherry for the fact that he would want to keep an eye on it. I mean, if he went off for several weeks he could come back and it wouldn't be there. Sunk, or something, so he would stop with it.'

Lack of wind could also be a hindrance. The boat would have to be moved by quanting it along. 'They used a pole, it were 20 to 24 ft long and I suppose an inch-and-a-half in diameter. About two-thirds of the way up it would start to taper off at each end. At one end you have a sort of a round knob, like a big wooden door knob, called a bott and at the other end an iron toe with a wooden bracket and that stops it going down into the mud. It sounds easier than it is, but you dig the bott into your shoulder, lean on it as hard as you can and walk along the deck, the plankways, and then once you get to the stern end you just pull it out and walk up to the forward end and then walk aft again. The plankways are usually 13 to 14 inches wide and then you had another 5 inch bit that stands up and that was painted so that you don't walk off the edge.'

Although hard work, quanting sets a romantic scene for the visitor, but it is the sails of the boats that really satisfy the artist's eye. However, the sails had to be well maintained, as Nigel explained. 'Sailcloth, years ago, that was cotton, quite a heavy cotton. On a pleasure wherry, because they were not sailing in the wintertime, it was untreated and left white. Now on a trading wherry, they leave it white the first year while she's stretching and then after that they would treat it with things like herring oil, paraffin and a drop of coal dust, all mixed up. The oil to preserve it and the coal dust to keep the mixture thick. Yeah, it would have been bloody dreadful, I bet, with your hands all covered with it. They would lay it on the grass and then slap that on one side and next year they would do the other side. The reason for doing it one side at a time was to prevent the sail getting too heavy with the weight of the oil and that on there. The weight would slow it up.

'The Lowestoft wherries, there weren't that many owned down there, but the few that there were, they used to have their sails treated where they used to have the fishing boats treated, so they were brown, but the others were black. They were treated with a different stuff. Cutch they call it, which is the same stuff as they used for the fishing boats. That's an oil-based stuff, but the ingredients bring it up brown instead of bringing it up black. The sail is heavy, if you have got to carry it anywhere, it would be heavy. I should think it would take a good half a dozen men to carry it.'

The life span of a wherry was about fifty years, perhaps lasting the length of the owner's working life, and during that time it was expected to have the sails replaced at least once. Nigel reckoned a new sail would have cost £70 in 1926, 'an awful lot of money in those times, an awful lot', but nevertheless, Uncle Billy didn't worry too much and often took a chance with his sail. He used to come through Haddiscoe on his way back from Lowestoft with a load of ice. 'He was on his own and he used to lock through the Mutford Lock and drop down in the harbour, all on his own, and work his way through the drifters that were down there blocking his way. He'd tie up on the quay there, load her up and then bring her back. Well, one day he was coming back and he was dropping down through Haddiscoe, and he'd go through the bridge, because there used to be a little, tiny bridge through Haddiscoe that used to lift up. Well, there's a big one there now, cars can go over and everything. What used to happen was that when a boat came along, the man would put out a great long pole with a sack on the end of it and you would drop in a shilling, or whatever the toll was, and he'd lift the bridge up, but my Uncle Billy always maintained that there was the right of navigation along there. I don't know whether he was right on that point actually, because that was a canal, they had dug that, it wasn't the river that was dug. It was the New Cut, the Haddiscoe Cut, so they might have been entitled to charge. That was dug for the shipping to get up to Norwich without going through Yarmouth, that was what it was all about, because Norwich was trying to be a port and Yarmouth was trying to be a port, so there was a bit of friction there, but it was a bit of a failure anyway. Well, my Uncle Billy, he used to come along with his sail up and he'd start hollering from about half a mile away, "Get the bridge open, I'm comin' through whether you do or you don't." And he would too, and the chap would say, "No, you gotta pay this time, we aren't havin' this every time you come along here." And Uncle Billy would come roaring down, yelling and hollaring at him to get the bridge open otherwise he would smash it up. Yes, he'd sail through it with all the gear up. Normally, you would have to lower everything down and I doubt you would have cleared that anyway because that was quite a low effort. He'd come along, "Get the bloody bridge open, I'm comin' along," the chap would shout, "NO, NO, NO, I aren't goin' to, you pay your shillin' and then I will." The chap would get really worried and winch it up at the last minute and Uncle Billy would roar past. I suppose he knew the chap would lift it up. If he didn't, being on his own, there was no way he would have got all his gear down in time. Apparently, when Uncle Billy died they went in his cabin and he had any amount of little lockers in there, and there was a locker full of little notes, summons from the Port and Haven for, "A boat gone through the bridge with all his gear up." He never did pay. He wouldn't pay.'

The masts of the wherries are also very heavy. Nigel has been recently working on the refurbishment of the *Solace,* which at 60 ft is the biggest of the remaining wherries. 'The mast weighs about 3 tons on there,' Nigel estimates, 'and it is 46 ft from pivot to top. When it's all weighted up properly, it's rigged up so that it pivots on top of the tabernacle which is the two bits of wood it sits on, so that when you are coming up to a bridge you lower the sail down and then lower the mast and when you've come through the bridge you let the mast come up again and then you hoist your sail again, all without stopping. Shooting a bridge, that's called.'

Regattas and races were all part of the wherryman's fun, as well as the local races they used to race off the coast once a year. 'Yes, this would be off Yarmouth,' Nigel confirms. 'Normally they'd just have the one sail, but for the races any old boats in the harbour would lend an old jib and they'd hoist it and they'd have two sails out. It was dangerous racing off the coast and my old friend, 'ole Jack Gedge was telling me, he remembers one, the bloody mast jumped up in the air, come forward a bit and smashed straight down through the whole boat. Of course, it didn't stay up much more after that. I can imagine the 'ole boy sitting aft, seeing this mast disappear through the boat. So that sunk her. Yes. So that's dangerous out there.'

Boats were sometimes built on speculation. Nigel had discovered that the *Solace* was built in this way by a firm called Hall's at Reedham in 1903. 'What they used to do was to build a hull, a wherry hull, and they wouldn't finish it off and if someone came along and said, we want a wherry that will hold 40 ton of gear, they would finish it off accordingly. Or, if they wanted a pleasure wherry, they would finish it off as a pleasure wherry. Well, she was a fine old boat and they used to race her. They used to roar about in her and they won the Wroxham Regatta ten times, ten years in a row. What they done to get *Solace* to go faster, because she was clinker-built, where the planks overlap, they thought they'd take that off the bottom, 'cos that slowed her up a bit and they had her cargo built which is where the planking is flush, smooth. So from the top, she looked as though she were clinker-built and from underneath she is cargo-built and that is why she was so good in the races. She can roar about because there is less resistance through the water on a cargo-built hull. Yes, she used to do well there.'

Nigel with a flag from a mast head.

At the top of the mast there is a flag of a particular construction. From a copper pivot extend two horizontal bars which hold a sheet of tin. This is perforated with a pattern and it has about 6 ft of silk bunting trailing from it, to flap about in the wind. From this the wherryman is able to read the wind's direction. There are three types of vane, first the 'gate vane' which might have a cut-out of the initial of the boat's name. 'On Uncle Billy's wherry, *Spray*, it was perforated with the letter "S", but old Jack Gedge's wherry, that had three stars like the belt of Orion, its namesake.' There is also the 'circular saw' vane. That was, of course, shaped like a circular saw and had a pattern cut out in the centre. '*The Hilda* had a Maltese Cross in hers, others might have had a star.' Lastly, there was the 'Jenny Morgan' vane for which Nigel has a particular fondness. 'This first appeared on *The Forget me-not* which was owned by my family. Early Jenny Morgan vanes were a Welsh woman holding a bunch of forget-me-nots. Well, after a while they got a bit bored with this, so she was changed. They were mostly women, there was one blowing a trumpet, but *Norfolk Hero* had Nelson at the top of the mast. In the wintertime they made the vanes a bit heavier than in the summertime, so in winter they would be made of tin or copper and in the summertime they would be a bit lighter, especially if they were racing. There's a poem about this. It goes:

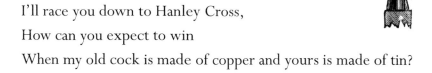

I'll race you down to Hanley Cross,
How can you expect to win
When my old cock is made of copper and yours is made of tin?

In spite of the dangers at sea for the wherries, which were usually built for sailing on the rivers and broads, the wherrymen would sometimes take chances and do a coasting trip. 'They used to if they wanted to get quick. They would go between Yarmouth and Lowestoft. If the wind and the sea were right they'd nip out the harbour and then nip in the other end, and if cargoes were scarce a group of boats would sail down to Southwold carrying bricks. Four or five of them actually sailed all the way down to Portsmouth when times were very hard.'

Most of the people who hired pleasure wherries did so simply to cruise the Broads, but occasionally, Nigel laughed, 'they would get a lot of hullaballoos down from London, you know, a group of lads hire a wherry for a week. There were no pianos on board as it was a real job to keep them in tune because of the damp, but they would come with banjos and things like that and go around causing mayhem for a week, but they would always have a crew, a steward and skipper with them so they were not dangerous.

'There was an old chap called Rats Bircham and he was a bit of a rum old stick. One Christmas he was dancing on the mantelpiece down at the pub. In those days they used sometimes to carry water in the old stone beer jars, the two gallon ones, and he was coming along the river from Aylesham where he was based and he sees this yacht coming along with all these hullaballoos on and they had all these crates of beer and he had his jars of water. "Ooh, I see you've got some beer on there and I've only got these stone jars of spirit. Say, will you swop?," he say, just like that, " 'cos I can't abide the stuff." "Yes, course we will, we'll do a swop." This was all while they were sailing towards each other and they worked out how much the deal was going to be. So, as they came alongside, they changed over, Rats handed over his jars of water which they thought was spirit and they handed over their beer. As they got apart, they took one swig and found out it was water and they all went mad. They were yelling and swearing at him, but he was big although he was short and they wouldn't have caught him anyway.

'Rats' boss at Aylesham used to get him to bring beer back with him sometimes because there were several breweries in Yarmouth. He used to say, "Don't you touch that beer in those jars." "I won't touch it," he say, and he be coming along there and every time he used to get thirsty he'd think of the beer sitting in this jar. "Oh, just one little drop won't hurt," and he'd pour himself out a mug and then when he'd drunk it, he'd dip his mug in the river and pour the water in there to fill it up again. And his boss, you know, he never cottoned on. Anyway one time, the silly old bugger, they were coming along and he took a couple of mugfuls out, sup, sup, dipped it in the river and filled it all back up nicely again. Next morning he was called into the office and the chap say, "Rats," he say, "what have you been doing drinking my beer?" "No master, I 'ent touched your beer. You know I'd never do a thing like. . . ." He say, "you silly old bugger, 'course you have, there's duckweed floating about in the top of it when I opened it up."

'In Norwich they had a factory where they made this stuff called "Wincannis". I believe it was sold as a tonic. Well, wherever that come from, they were carrying it in its raw state and that was real old jollop. Well, they got thirsty and they thought, "We've got that old Wincannis tonic in there, we'll have a drop of that." So, they broached a whole barrel. Yeah, tasted all right, so the two of them emptied this bloody barrel of this stuff and the next day they couldn't get up out of bed and they were really ill and they were laid up for a week. They couldn't walk or anything. Gosh, they felt bad through drinking this old tonic. Imagine the owners of the wherries at that time of day. They must have known what they were like, must have done. Yeah, 'cos Rats always sailed for other people.

'Uncle Billy sailed his wherry on his own up 'til he was seventy-two and that was bloody good going for a 40-ton wherry, carting ice and timber from Colman's deal ground. The big coasters used to come in from the Baltic full of deal boards and he would load *Spray* up and then bring that back to Norwich. He worked damned hard he did, really hard. He was very skilled too. He were over at Breydon once, that's all

Billy with Prince in the ferry boat, 1933. (Michael Seago Collection)

that's left of the estuary at Yarmouth now, and that is about four miles long and a mile wide, with posts for a channel. You couldn't see the posts or anything, it was so misty and murky. Well, he got across somehow or other. I don't know how the hell he done it. That was spoken about, that he had done this, and that was thought fairly well of, that he crept across there. Well, anyway, come seventy-two, his two remaining boys said, "You know you gotta pack up now because you are getting old. Pack it up." Well, he didn't want to, but he finally agreed. And what he used to do then! There's The Farriers, in King Street, that's a public house, and near there is where he had his boat sheds and he did the ferry there. He had a little ol', whatsay? Bit like a Broad's punt really, double-ended clinker built, little dinghy thing, and he used to load that up with people who wanted to nip across the river. It was like when he was on his bloody wherry. He used to load it up so much, these people, they used to be frightened. They hardly dare breathe because there was too little freeboard left on it. They were really that cramped up. Nevermind, he earned an extra few bob.'

Billy must have missed the excitement of 'truckin' and tradin' and it proved just too much to give that up completely. 'Well, what he used to do at night-time, he'd go along these Dutch coasters and nick the coal and he'd come back and put it in his sheds and then he'd sell it; "truckin' and tradin'", you see. Well, one night Aunt Polly was up waiting at home for him to arrive and he didn't show up and they wondered where he was. Well, he was normally back fairly late at night, but he weren't even back then and she got wind up. So she went and saw the boys, "Your father 'ent back yet, you'd better go see the old manager down at General Steam Navigation." He was a friend of theirs who ran wherries. "Go and see him and see if he can sort something out." So they done that. They went and saw him and he said, "Right, well, let's go and see if we can find him." Well, they couldn't see him on the river, they found the boat and it was full of sacks of coal, but they didn't know where he was.

"Well, there's only one place where he can be, that's down ol' police station." So they went in and he was sitting up one corner and he had his little 'ole white dawg there and the policeman couldn't get near him because the dog was keeping him away. Uncle Billy was saying, "Do what you like, but it's no good fining me because I can't give nothing, because I've got nothing to give." The policemen were all laughing, because it was a bit of a joke really because he was up in his eighties then, you see. Well, this was all going on and the ol' chap from Steam Navigation say, "Now, you've got this old boy, now what's he going to do? He ain't gonna do a runner, is he? Just let him go home and then go in the morning and sort it out." Now they didn't really think that was quite the thing to do, but in the end he persuaded them. They said they ought to keep him in the cells overnight, but they had the coal as evidence and there was no way he could get out of it. So they let him go home. "And for God's sake, take that bloody nuisance of a dawg with you!"

"So off he went, but he didn't go straight home. What he done was, he went down to his little rowing boat. Now when they'd built this quay where he moored his wherry, instead of the quay going straight down, they had built a concrete rampart, right under the water so a boat could float over it. It was like a concrete ledge under the water. What he done was, he took this little ol' boat alongside the wherry and he emptied his sacks of coal underneath the wherry on to this concrete ledge and then hid the sacks up. Anyway, then he went home. They were a bit worried, but not too worried, sort of thing. Next morning old Inspector came round. "Billy," he say, "well, we're sorry, but we don't really want to do anything, but we've got the coal." Billy say, "What bloody coal?" "Well, the coal in your boat as evidence." "Don't know what you're on about." So finally they went down there, to the boat. Of course, that was empty. This bloke went light, he was bloody furious. "The bloody buggers have let you out and now we haven't got the stuff." "Don't know what you're on about," say Billy. Well, they couldn't do anything because they had lost the evidence. Anyway, he left it a few months and they had what you call an ice-dydle, which is a long pole with a hoop on the end with a net on it, and after a couple of months they just stood on the quay just dydling the coal out again.'

Uncle Billy died in 1936 when he was eighty-six years old. He tripped over when unloading illicit coal from a Dutch boat, 'So he was a bit black,' remarked Nigel. 'Probably taking it into his house, because he had a storeroom in there for all the stuff he nicked. Once he had caught a cold taking a bath and had to have two days off work, so he decided he wouldn't ever bathe again. Aunt Polly was horrified. "I aren't having him buried like that. He aren't going to meet the good Lord looking like that." So they got him on the old table and scrubbed him from head to toe! Poor ol' boy.'

The wherrymen had kept going in spite of the railways, the new roads and the abundance of lorries made available by army surplus, but it was when his wherry was motorized that another old wherryman, Jack Gedge, was really upset. Jack, who had been a good friend of Nigel's, died when he was 102 years old and Nigel obviously has a lot of sympathy for him. 'He stood on Allen's Yard and cried when they pulled his wherry out and took all the gear off it. You see that was his pride and joy and they got that bloody great auger bit and rammed it up the old wherry's arse and started windin' it round and going through the timber and all this wood was turnin' out and it upset him so much he started to cry because it was ruinin' his boat. On the other hand, he knew if he didn't keep it up he'd never do any more work.

'The wherrymen were thought of badly, really, and when they came in, people would certainly think, we've got to be a bit careful now and watch what's about. They lived so hard and so terribly, that they got a bad name in the villages. Funny really, because people romanticize about it, and that, now and that does annoy me, because people don't realize the hard graft that went behind it. How hard it was, and it bloody was, you know.'